Keys to Faster Learning

The Science That Makes Learning
More Fun and Even Easy!

Dr. Linda Ross-Happy

Dedication
and Special Thanks

With deepest gratitude to my two very special Gary's. My brother, Gary, who if he hadn't become a highly successful professional musician, could easily have been an editor with his sharp eye and keen intellect. And to my beloved late husband, Gary, who often had to remind me to "Go Write!" I am so grateful to him for loving me, encouraging me and always supporting me.

Special Thanks to all my friends who have lifted me up and sustained me during the publishing of this book, especially Larry F. Levenson through his photography and insightful suggestions, and Dr. Paul Jones who worked tirelessly to assist me with the final format. I deeply appreciate all of you.

"The illiterate of the future will not be the person who cannot read. It will be the person who does not know how to learn."

—Alvin Toffler
American Writer and Futurist

Table of Contents

Introduction

This is a book about learning — learning how to learn. We spend so much time in school, studying, reading, researching, listening to lectures, etc., but how much time or interest is given to the main tool — the major device we use in learning — the brain? Few of us have received instructions on how to utilize the brain to maximize the learning process. Oh sure, we may have been given tips on how to take notes, the best way to organize materials for study, and all that, but I'm talking about the brain itself. What do we really know? I think for the most part, we know very little about how the brain operates and how to use it. That's what we're going to be doing in this book — taking a look at how the brain operates and how we can utilize that knowledge to make learning faster and easier than ever before. At the outset, I'd like to state that this is undoubtedly the most exciting — actually thrilling — time in terms of brain discoveries. The last twenty years have seen an explosion in brain research, and the findings

have essentially turned what we previously believed about the brain on its ear. New studies in neurogenesis have illuminated the brain's ability to grow and develop new cells. This would have been regarded as absurd only a few decades ago when the common belief was that the brain was the only organ in the body incapable of creating new cells. Neuroscientists have even discovered the brain's capacity to rewire itself following an injury and to create new pathways —essentially to heal itself. But it goes even further. Studies in the last 30 years have focused on what has come to be known as neuroplasticity, which is the brain's ability to continually form new neural connections and even reorganize itself in response to new situations. This research is showing that learning — learning a new language, learning a new skill, learning to play a musical instrument, any kind of learning — increases the neural connections in the brain. So, in other words, in the process of learning, you're not only changing your brain, but you are also increasing your brain's capacity to learn! This is exciting stuff! In fact, many researchers believe that no one has even come close to using the full, maximum capacity of his or her brain! We are being told that the brain is indeed miraculous and quite possibly limited only by our beliefs! So what does this mean for us? Everything! It means we don't have to stay stuck with the idea that we're slow at learning, or that learning is difficult. In means that even if we've failed in the past, perhaps even failed miserably, it doesn't have to be that way again. It means that we don't even have to pay homage to an I.Q. Score that labeled and limited us. In fact, ample evidence supports

the fact that by understanding how your brain functions and applying that knowledge in ways that enable you to use your brain more effectively, I.Q. scores can indeed be changed. You see, you are being given the opportunity here to change your learning patterns in profound and dramatic ways. Learning how the brain works and putting that information to work is going to require you to open yourself up to some new ways of thinking about learning. Some of it may even seem ridiculous at first. But I ask you to suspend judgement. Go through all the exercises presented here and give it a real try. Give it a chance. Because if you work at it diligently and persistently, you will surprise yourself at how easily you are able to learn faster. Much of the material in this book I wrote over twenty years ago to acquaint my university students with the latest discoveries in learning techniques at the time. That book was entitled, The Student Guide to Accelerated Learning, and all of that information still remains valid today. This revised and expanded book differs from the previous book in two primary ways. First, in addition to the learning techniques presented in my original book — many of which were considered quite revolutionary at the time — I have included some of the incredible findings in brain research since then that have dramatically increased our understanding of how we learn. Second, although my original book was written for university students, this book is designed for everyone — that is, everyone who desires to learn faster. I think it is clear to all of us, that learning is not simply the task of students in formal school situations, but that it is increasingly being required

for all of us to continue learning beyond the classroom. Thomas Paine had this figured out in 1794 when he wrote: "As to the learning that any person gains from school education, it serves only like a small capital, to put him in the way of beginning learning for himself afterwards." So it's always been true, perhaps, but now it is vital. As the world changes, as technology advances, as information increases exponentially, we see and understand that we must continue learning throughout our lifetimes.

It's going to be an exciting adventure together as we explore the brain and how to use it to dramatically increase our learning potential. I promise if you keep an open mind, diligently practice the exercises, and commit yourself to a new way of thinking and learning, you will astound yourself in your newfound ability to learn easier and faster. So let's get started discovering and using The Keys to Faster Learning!

Chapter 1

Introducing Your Brain

How much do you really know about your brain? I ask you that because as we are beginning this adventure in understanding and utilizing the "Keys to Faster Learning," it's important for you to have at least a nodding acquaintance with just exactly how powerful, mysterious, and miraculous your brain actually is. So let's briefly take a look.

Just the Facts

Consider this fact: It is estimated that the brain contains 10 billion — 10,000,000,000 — neurons, the nerve cells that process and transfer information. One neuron is capable of making over 10,000 connections with other cells, and the number of synapses (the tiny gaps through which information is transferred) in the brain is estimated at 10 trillion, that's 10,000,000,000,000! I mean, come on, that's a lot of capacity!!

Keep that in mind while you consider this from Peter Russell's *The Brain Book*:

> It is frequently stated that we use only 10 percent of our full mental potential. This, it now appears, is rather an overestimate. We probably do not use even 1 percent — more likely 0.1 percent or less. The apparent limits of the human brain are only the limits of the uses to which we put it, and the limits of what we believe is possible.[1]

One could interpret this to mean that we use only a small percentage of the actual grey matter or area of the brain, and that the other 99 percent or more must be lying dormant. But on further reflection, I think this reference to using such a small percentage of the brain has more to do with the fact that we are so inefficient in using our brain's capabilities. So much more is possible. We have enormously greater potential. We just haven't figured out how to tap into this vast unused potential.

But it gets even better and more intriguing. New research has discovered another facet of the brain that seems almost unbelievable — "neuroplasticity." The term is derived from "neuro" for neuron and "plastic" for changeable, and refers to the process by which the brain actually changes itself. Dr. Norman Doidge, psychiatrist and researcher at Columbia University, has described his experiences with this phenomenon in his fascinating book, *The Brain That Changes Itself*:

In the course of my travels I met a scientist who enabled people who had been blind since birth to begin to see, another who enabled the deaf to hear; I spoke with people who had had strokes decades before and had been declared incurable, who were helped to recover with neuroplastic treatments; I met people whose learning disorders were cured and whose IQs were raised; I saw evidence that it is possible for eighty-year-olds to sharpen their memories to function the way they did when they were fifty-five.[2]

The blind learning to see? Learning disorders cured? IQ's being raised? Preposterous! History and long years of medical experts tell us this is impossible! Doidge himself acknowledges this:

For four hundred years this venture would have been inconceivable because mainstream medicine and science believed that brain anatomy was fixed. The common wisdom was that after childhood the brain changed only when it began the long process of decline; that when brain cells failed to develop properly, or were injured, or died, they would not be replaced. Nor could the brain ever alter its structure and find a new way to function if part of it was damaged.[3]

But thankfully we are no longer stuck with that centuries-old belief system regarding the brain and its limitations. Not only that, researchers are discovering that the brain is capable of so much more than we ever thought possible. That's what this brain plasticity business is all about. Dr. Michael Merzenich, a professor emeritus and neuroscientist at the University of California San Francisco, and the person described as the world's leading researcher in brain plasticity, believes we can actually change the very capacity of the brain and increase our abilities to learn.

Here's how Doidge describes this idea:

> Merzenich claims that when learning occurs in a way consistent with the laws that govern brain plasticity, the mental "machinery" of the brain can be improved so that we learn and perceive with greater precision, speed, and retention.[4]

This is exciting stuff!! Why? Because it means we're not limited. No matter what you may have thought about your learning abilities in the past — how dumb you were or smart you were — you don't have to be or feel limited. Everything we knew or believed in the past about our brain's functioning and abilities has to be reexamined. With this new understanding of the brain, our capacity for learning and for changing, and even growing the brain, may be virtually limitless!

This means you know longer are justified in declaring that learning is difficult for you, or that you're not very bright. You may have thought that or believed that in the past, but in our time together we will be breaking free of every one of those limiting chains that might have held you in the past.

The starting place for our adventure in exploring the wonderful *Keys to Faster Learning* is understanding and knowing that your capacity for learning is limitless.

O━━▼ Key 1: Your brain has a far greater capacity for learning than you ever dreamed possible. The latest research indicates we can improve and grow our brains for even faster and easier learning.
Remember this and never allow yourself to feel limited.

The Left and Right of It

Are you aware that you actually possess two brains in one? This incredible brain of yours is divided into a right and a left hemisphere which is connected by a network of nerve fibers called the corpus callosum through which information is transmitted. It's not my intention for this book to delve into a lot of brain anatomy and physiology, but I think it's important for you to be aware of these two hemispheres of your brain and how they function, to help you understand and utilize your brain's potential to the fullest. Let's start with a little background.

The discovery of the two brain hemispheres is largely attributed to Dr. Roger Sperry who received the Nobel Prize in 1981 for his brain research in the 1960's. Dr. Sperry performed brain surgeries on epileptic patients in which he severed the corpus callosum (that band of nerve fibers joining the two hemispheres) in an attempt to control their seizures. Studies of Dr. Sperry's recovering patients at the California Institute of Technology led to the realization that the two hemispheres are capable of operating independently of each other and that the two hemispheres process information in different ways.

As revolutionary as Sperry's work may have seemed at the time, the ancient Egyptians were also aware of the two brain hemispheres and the fact that the left hemisphere of the brain controls the right side of the body, and vice versa. This is supported by the fact that a stroke, or damage to the left hemisphere of the brain will most seriously affect the right side of the body, and the left side of the body is affected when the right side of the brain is damaged.

Left Brain/ Right Brain Specialization

Brain researchers have concluded that distinctively contrasting modes of thinking exist between the right and left-brain hemispheres. For our purposes, and to get a better grasp of what this means, we'll list a few words to describe the contrasting ways in which the two brain hemispheres process information in the following chart:

Left Brain	Right Brain
Words	Pictures
Speech	Feelings
Logic	Images
Details	Symbols
Numbers	Music

As you can see from the chart, the left brain prefers to operate in terms of the logical and the factual. It is comfortable in dealing with bits of information and separating the whole of an element into its operative parts. It also tends to proceed in a step by step, orderly fashion and is our main hemisphere for speech.

The right hemisphere, on the other hand, enjoys seeing likenesses and relationships. It takes in the whole of a situation instantaneously and cannot be bothered with the details. Life is patterns and shapes all happening at once, and it tends to feel rather than talk.

We may be oversimplifying this a bit, but I hope it enables you to get an idea of the distinctively different modes of thinking in the two brain hemispheres. Now, in keeping with those different styles of thinking, the two brain hemispheres exhibit contrasting areas of specialization. Let's look at a few examples of how the two brain hemispheres specialize differently:

Left Brain	Right Brain
Good with numbers	Uses imagination and pictures
Keeps track of time	Lacks a sense of time
Communicates with words	Communicates with gestures, pictures, and music

In general, we may say that that the left-brain hemisphere generates our factual and verbal abilities, and the right hemisphere is the origin of our artistic, intuitive, and emotional aspects. This difference in brain hemisphere functions is particularly evidenced by the fact that a stroke, or damage to the left hemisphere, often affects one's speech but does not affect the ability to sing; right hemispheric damage often results in the loss of musical abilities but not in the ability to speak.

What does all this mean to us? Let's look further.

Revering the Left Brain

We don't have to look far to see that our Western system of education, with its emphasis on the logical, analytical, step by step thinking process, is heavily biased toward the left-brain mode of thinking. In fact, historically our society has emphasized the superiority of logical thinking and factual learning and tended to regard right-brain creativity and artistic endeavors as more or less entertaining and diversionary. I was made particularly aware of this when a prominent brain surgeon confessed to me that he is far less nervous about operating on the right hemisphere of the brain than on the left hemisphere. But neglecting the functions of the right-brain hemisphere is utilizing only half of our mental capacity. And further, in certain situations, which we'll discuss in greater detail later, the left brain can in many ways interfere with one's performance and creativity.

Right-Brain Dreamers

Stories abound of many of the greatest men and women throughout history who were unsuccessful in school because there were "dreamers" — a term often applied to a person who is right-dominant in his or her thinking process. The classic example is Thomas Edison, who latest three months in school and was criticized by his teacher for being a dreamy boy who paid little attention to his books or his teacher. The story goes that his teacher reported him to the visiting inspector for being unlike the other boys and suggested that it was a waste of time to keep him in school. This may be the reason Edison was consistently critical of formal education and professed that the only education of any value was the one we acquire for ourselves. Perhaps the fact that Edison's only education was through reading and being privately tutored by his mother allowed him to develop his right-brain creative mode of thinking, and ultimately become the greatest inventor of all time.

Walt Disney didn't last in school, and neither did Buckminster Fuller. This is quite interesting when one considers that these men are perhaps two of the most creative thinkers in recent history!

And consider these quotes from school reports describing Dominic O'Brien, the Eight-Time World Memory Champion: "He tends to dream in the middle of a calculation, which leads him to lose track of the thought." "Unless Dominic really shakes himself up and gets down to work, he is not going to achieve any success . . . He is painfully slow."[5] Yet, this right-brain dreamer now has an entry in the Guinness Book of Records for memorizing a random sequence of 2808 playing cards!

Developing the Right Brain

If you've been criticized for being a dreamer, having your "head in the clouds," or simply being "out of touch," you are more than likely right brain dominant in your thinking processes. But now, rather than feeling bad about those criticisms, which often go along with having that imagination, you can concentrate on making all that right-brain power work for you instead of against you. When you understand how to utilize your creative energies, supporting them with the analytical and systematic thinking of the left brain, you can develop your ability to learn and retain information beyond anything you have previously experienced. In other words, you can harness the techniques of faster learning!

If you've never been much of a dreamer and wondered at times whether or not you've got any imagination at all, you are undoubtedly left-brain dominant. Many of the imaging exercises in this book are specifically designed for you and will dramatically strengthen the thought processes of your right brain. In this way, your left-brain logic can be enhanced by creative inspiration. As you tap into this creative side of your nature, which by the way has just been waiting for you to recognize and utilize it, you'll awaken an artist within that you probably didn't even realize you had. You will be able to open an entirely new dimension of thinking where ideas and insights greet you at every turn, and in the process, utilize all of the keys to faster learning.

Expanded Thinking

So you see, we don't need to get into a debate over which type of thinking (logical left-brain versus creative right-brain) is superior. Our goal is a kind of whole-brain thinking where the thought processes of each hemispheric mode enhances those of the other. The creative and intuitive insight of the right-brain imagination and the logical, step-by-step calculations of the left brain working together to make learning faster, easier, and yes, even fun! If you are willing to try some new ideas, work with the exercises, and keep an open mind, your ability to learn faster and easier might just astound you!

O—— Key 2: Integrating the logical and analytical thinking of the left brain with the creative and imaginative capacities of the right brain results in whole-brain thinking.

Engage both sides of your brain to dramatically enhance your learning abilities.

Chapter 2

The Psychological Side of Learning

So if our brains truly have unlimited potential, what is it that holds us back? What is it that is keeping you or me or any other person from learning and achieving at the level of genius? The answer rests squarely within ourselves. It is our own beliefs. What we think and feel about our learning abilities, backed up by the evidence of achievements and failures of the past, powerfully influences what we are able to do, learn, and accomplish in the present. Hundreds of research studies in practically every area of learning and performance have proven this beyond a doubt. But before we discuss this further, let's take a quick assessment of what this might mean for you.

How Smart Are You?

I think you can answer this question fairly easily. We all have a kind of set, inner attitude about our learning abilities

— one that we've probably carried with us throughout our lives so far. This inner attitude is intensely personal, and I doubt many of us would dare mention it to another. Even so, for our purposes here, let's see if we can take a closer look at this inner attitude by getting it out there in black and white.

Without any soul-searching or debate, quickly go over the five statements below and write down, if possible, which word in bold print better describes you. The word may not exactly describe you, but which of the two seems closer?

1. In general, I learn **faster/slower** than other people.
2. Other people usually regard me as a **sharp/slow** learner.
3. I find learning new material is **easy/difficult**.
4. I think taking exams is **challenging/terrifying**.
5. People don't know that I secretly feel **smart/stupid**.

Now look at all five words. Which way did you lean? Are you more inclined to think of yourself as a fast learner or a slow learner? Do you think of yourself as smart or stupid? Your answers probably didn't surprise you. As we said, most people have a pretty good idea of what they believe about themselves in the brain department. We're just highlighting this powerful state of inner belief here as a point of departure.

For those of you who already believe you are smart and find learning easy and fun, the exercises and techniques we will study are going to enhance your learning abilities even further. Your attempts to learn faster are going to be very effective and you will surprise yourself at how you are able to learn with even greater mastery.

If, however, you tend to believe, for whatever reason, that you are a slow learner, we're going to systematically set out to change those beliefs and set you on a course where learning will not only be easier but fun. Negative and limiting beliefs can be changed through diligent and conscious reprogramming of your thought processes. It isn't easy, but the results are so phenomenal that it's certainly worth any amount of effort you're able to give it. You don't have to stay stuck with limiting beliefs. You also don't need to take my word for it. As you practice some of the exercises we'll discuss, and begin meeting with greater and increasingly more successes, you'll prove it to yourself. You'll see. It's very exciting!

The Power of Beliefs

I'd like you to consider this real-life example of just how powerfully and dramatically beliefs can influence a person's abilities. The story concerns the outstanding feat of the Russian weight lifter, Vasily Alexeyev, and is detailed in the book, *Superlearning*. Alexeyev was told by his trainers during a weight-lifting event that the weight he would be lifting was his world record of 499.9 pounds. In actuality, the weight was 501.5 pounds — rather an awesome load when one considers that for years the common belief was that 500 pounds was the unsurpassable barrier in weight lifting. So, you might ask, he was fooled into believing the weight was 499.9 pounds when it was really 501.5 pounds? Exactly! Not only did Alexeyev break the 500- pound barrier by lifting 501.5 pounds, he later went on to lift 564 pounds at the Olympics and set 80 world records in weight lifting![6]

You may have what you consider unsurpassable barriers when it comes to learning, though let's assume they weigh less than 500 pounds. But whatever your blocks or hindrances may be — or seem to be — see if you can put them aside for awhile as we explore what just may be possible for you. Let's continue.

Negative Beliefs

Not only are beliefs powerful, but negative beliefs can also sabotage our best efforts. This was pointed out in a fascinating study which showed how the influence of negative beliefs can affect performance in a most unusual way. Jim Fannin, who is a consultant and mental coach for some of the world's top athletes, describes in his book, *S.C.O.R.E. For Life*, an experiment he created involving children and their perceptions of their own running abilities. Children were told if they were fast, they should go to one side of the gym, and if they were slow, not fast, they should go to the other side of the gym. Next, they tested each child's speed while running the 40yard dash. The children were not told their speeds, even though some of the "slow" kids ran faster than the ones who had grouped themselves with the fast kids. Listen to Fannin's account of what happened next:

> The group was reassembled into the original groups of fast and slow kids. Then we announced that the slow kids wanted to race the fast kids. The slow kids looked stunned. We then paired up one-on-one races between the "fast" and the "slow" kids. Many of the "slower" kids were faster than the "faster" kid that they were paired with. The child who thought he was slow but in fact ran the fastest sprinted into the lead 98 percent of the time. But then the kids' mental hardwiring took over, and with only 10 yards to go in the race, the same kid that thought he or she was slow slowed down and lost the race, holding true to their belief and expectations. This occurred 92 percent of the time.[7]

Think about it. Could that be you? Not succeeding, not excelling, not winning whatever race you're running simply because you believe you can't? Could it be that you've essentially been sabotaging yourself? You may not believe it, at least not yet, but just give yourself a chance to think about it.

Let's delve further into the power of negative beliefs by looking at how others may be affecting us, perhaps without even knowing it.

Limiting Beliefs of Others

We may understand and accept the fact that our beliefs have the power to dictate our strengths and level of abilities, but did you ever stop to think that the beliefs of others can also have an influential effect on us? I think most of us realize the profound affect our parents can and have had on all aspects of our lives, including our learning abilities. However, a more subtle, and perhaps even more insidious influence on our learning abilities can be conveyed by our teachers.

Consider this as described by Peter Russell in *The Brain Book*:

> If a group of children is divided into two groups of equal aptitudes but their teachers are told that children in one group have high IQs and are expected to excel at school whereas the other children are academically poor, the first group will do much better than the second. This effect, known as the Pygmalion effect, has been borne out by numerous studies, not only in school, but in business, psychiatry, medicine, politics, social relationships, and other situations.[8]

I find some of these studies heartbreaking — especially when teachers, who have dedicated their lives to helping children learn, may be the very ones preventing those children from learning without even realizing it.

Statistics and Beliefs

Of the many ways and situations in which we acquire negative and limiting beliefs, it seems to me that looking at statistics — those irrefutable facts and figures — may present us with a set of beliefs that can be the most difficult to overcome. After all, statisticians with their data derived from carefully constructed research projects give us information on what is possible and what is impossible, or highly improbable, and we must agree. Or must we? Research now indicates that what we believe about those statistics has an even greater power over us than the numbers themselves.

Dr. David Hamilton talks about the power of beliefs and statistics in his thought-provoking book, *How Your Mind Can Heal Your Body*. Although much of this book deals with healing and the body, this account is particularly worthy of our consideration:

> It's even been proven that what you believe affects your academic performance. A 2006 study published in the journal Science examined the mathematics scores of 220 female students who had each read one of two different fake research reports. Half of the girls read one report claiming that scientists had discovered genes on the Y chromosome (that only men have) that gave males a 5 percent advantage over females in mathematics. The other half read a bogus paper that asserted that men had a 5 percent advantage only because of the way teachers stereotyped girls and

boys at an early age. When the students were tested, the group who believed that the difference was just stereotyping — and therefore felt that they were just as good at mathematics as men were — did much better than the one made up of girls who *thought* they had a genetic disadvantage.[9]

So you see, you don't have to allow a set of statistics to hold power over you, your abilities, or what you are able to achieve. I'm not doubting the validity of statistics, mind you — absolutely not. But I do know that your belief in yourself and your ideas about what you can and cannot do have the ability to transcend any set of statistics.

In my own life, what I consider my two most meaningful and important accomplishments would never have become reality if I had heeded the statistics available at the time. You see, these accomplishments were considered highly unlikely for me — according to the statistics.

If the statistics look good for you and predict great success — fantastic!! Print them on huge poster board and hang them on the wall! But if the statistics indicate great difficulties, the probability of an unfavorable outcome, anything less than success — ignore it. You have better things to do, like go out there and succeed!

Changing Limiting Beliefs

As we've discussed, you don't have to be stuck with any statistics that prove you can't be, do, or have what you desire. But let's take it further. You don't have to stay stuck with any limiting beliefs. Why? Because it's possible to change those beliefs and in so doing, open ourselves up to an unlimited potential that we've possibly never known before. I won't say it's easy, but it can be done.

Remember Dominic O'Brien, the Eight-Time World Memory Champion whose teachers described him as "slow?" Listen to what he says about the power of belief when he began memorizing entire decks of playing cards to match and even surpass the feats of the great mnemonist, Creighton Carvello:

> When I realized where I'd been going wrong, and — most importantly — how to fix it, I had a stratospheric surge in self-belief, like the alchemist turning common elements into gold. It was all the incentive I needed to practice hard, working at deck after deck of cards, until my memory could do the same and more as Creighton Carvello. It's this self-belief that I think transformed me — far more than codes or decks of cards — and taught me that anything is achievable with a will and a way, something my schooldays had singularly failed to do."[10]

Yes, a belief in oneself is powerful, and you can achieve it by transforming those negative beliefs into positive ones. It isn't even necessary to spend time identifying the origin of our negative beliefs — in fact, why bother? We're spending our energy and efforts now on defining ourselves as having unlimited brain power and greater potential than we realized. The exercises in this book are designed to get us there. We're setting our minds to the goal of learning faster and easier. With attention, a certain amount of effort, and practice, we'll prove our abilities in ways that just might have once seemed impossible.

Key 3: Our own beliefs powerfully determine how fast we are able to learn. Deliberately change negative and limiting beliefs about your learning abilities to positive ones that will enable you to learn with ease and confidence — often in ways you never thought possible.

Chapter 3

The Physical Side of Learning

As mysterious and complicated as the workings of the brain may be, it is still a physical organ and improving your physical condition can and does improve the brain's functioning. Oddly, for many of us, this aspect of an optimally functioning brain is often ignored and even neglected. But if we're going to truly kick the brain into faster learning, we need to understand this and focus on making sure the brain is operating at its highest level. So it's worth our time here to consider some of the contributing physical factors that affect the brain and its ability to operate at peak performance.

Exercise

You've probably been lectured about the benefits of exercise, and you already know that physical exercise is a huge component in one's overall health. But in our attempts to learn faster, it's important for us to understand how essential exercise is to the brain's functioning at its highest level. Let's look at some of the reasons why.

Exercise and Oxygen

"Although the brain makes up only about 2% of the body's total weight, it utilizes 25% of the oxygen we take in."[11] Serious and often irreversible damage to the brain occurs after only a few minutes of oxygen deprivation. The brain simply requires oxygen to function at its best. Research also indicates that the brain utilizes even more oxygen during times of study or concentration. So we need to be sure we are getting an adequate supply. And as you probably already know, the best way to increase the supply of oxygen to the brain is through exercise. During exercise, the heart rate speeds up, and the flow of oxygen-rich blood is increased in our body, including the brain. We can think of this increase in oxygen as actually nourishing the brain in ways that allow it to function better.

But this increase in oxygen to the brain through exercise is encouraged in an even further way. In his book, *Brain Rules*, John Medina, who is the director of the Brain Center for Applied Learning Research at Seattle Pacific University, describes how exercise increases the blood vessels in your brain. He compares this increase of blood vessels to the building of new roads which allows your brain greater access to oxygen and food.[12] The stuff we need for optimal learning!

Exercise and Biological Changes

The fact that exercise increases blood vessels in the brain indicates that exercise creates biological changes in the brain. That's quite astounding when you think about it. But there's more. Harvard Professor of Psychiatry, Dr. John Ratey, emphasizes this fact in his fascinating book, *Spark: The Revolutionary New Science of Exercise and the Brain:* "The more neuroscientists discover about this process, the clearer it becomes that exercise provides an unparalleled stimulus, creating an environment in which the brain is ready, willing, and able to learn."[13]

That's great! We exercise more, we feel better, and best of all, the brain is enabled to function at higher levels. But what about the lack of exercise? Dr. Ratey talks about that too in a somewhat alarmingly way: "What's even more disturbing, and what virtually no one recognizes, is that inactivity is killing our brains too — physically shriveling them."[14]

Shriveling our brains?! It may be time to think seriously about getting more exercise if you haven't been doing so!

Exercise and Learning in Action

While all these exercise statements may be intriguing, let's look at an actual study of physical exercise and its impact on the classroom. Naperville (a city west of Chicago) District 203 has conducted a study which involved 19,000 students on the impact of exercise and performance in the classroom. Students are required to attend a Zero Hour PE Class, as in 7:10 a.m. Prior to the start of classes to find out whether rigorous workouts before school improves reading ability along with other subjects. What they've found has been remarkable. Test scores improved, students' self-images were strengthened, along with other amazing results. Dr. Ratey describes it as follows: "It's no coincidence that, academically, the district consistently ranks among the state's top ten, even though the amount of money it spends on each pupil — considered by educators to be a clear predictor of success — is notably lower than other top-tier Illinois public schools."[15]

It's also interesting to note in this study that a group of literacy students were divided into two classes, one of which took place during second period and the other during eighth period. The experimenters were not surprised to find that the students in the second-period class, which was closer to the exercise workout, performed better than the students in the 8th period class.[16]

What we can take from this, is not only can we learn faster when we're engaged in a strenuous exercise program, but that our learning abilities appear to be greater immediately following the exercise, while we're still feeling its effects.

Fertilizer for the Brain

A dramatic change in how researchers viewed the

working of the brain occurred with the discovery of a protein known as brain-derived neurotrophic factor (BDNF). No, we're not going to go into an in-depth study of this brain protein. The important thing for us to know, is <u>how</u> BDNF affects the brain. Dr Ratey describes BDNF as a kind of fertilizer for the brain — he even calls it Miracle-Gro for the brain. These are his words: "Early on, researchers found that if they sprinkled BDNF onto neurons in a petri dish, the cells automatically sprouted new branches, producing the same structural growth required for learning — and causing me to think of BDNF as Miracle-Gro for the brain."[17]

So how do we get more of this brain fertilizer? You guessed it — Exercise! The first researcher to link exercise to an increase in BDNF, this Miracle-Gro for the brain, was Carl Cotman, director of the Institute for Brain Aging and Dementia at the University of California, Irvine, with his study on mice. Not only did Cotman's brain scans of mice who exercised by running show an increase in BDNF over the control mice (the ones who didn't run), but those who ran farther had even higher levels BDNF.

No, it's not just in mice. A group of German researchers in a 2007 study determined that people learned vocabulary words 20% faster following exercise than they did before exercise, and it was directly related to increased levels of BDNF.[18] So if exercise actually increases a protein that acts like a fertilizer for the brain, causing the cells to sprout new branches, we should think seriously about how important exercise is to learning.

I like the way Dr. Ratey, after all his research, sums it up so succinctly, "What it means is that you have the power to change your brain. All you have to do is lace up your running shoes."[19]

🔑 **Key 4: Exercise boosts brain power!! Engage in physical exercise to nourish and grow you brain, and learn faster!**

Sleep

We often hear how important it is to get enough sleep, but the fact is that adequate sleep is absolutely essential if we want to have a brain that is functioning at its best. Furthermore, lack of sleep has been determined to contribute to a plethora of medical conditions including heart disease, depression, high blood pressure, diabetes, and on and on. So, even beyond the learning factor, sleep is vitally important to maintain our health and sense of well-being. That's just basic. Having stated that, let's examine more specifically how sleep affects the brain.

Sleep Before and After Learning

Sleep deprivation impairs our ability to take in new information and impairs our ability to process that information. A brain that is fatigued has trouble paying attention and focusing on the learning task at hand. Whether you're reading, attending a lecture, practicing a new skill, or learning a musical score, the tired brain cannot and does not function at its best.

That might seem obvious to you — more like common sense. But did you realize that the brain also requires sleep <u>after</u> learning? That's right. The brain has work to do after the learning event to get the information into a stable and useful form for you. This isn't something you have to do. It's not a matter of you having to continue to go over and over the information. No, the brain simply needs to go through a process of organizing the information and it knows how to do that. What it needs for <u>you</u> to do at this point is to sleep, so that it can get the job done more efficiently. During sleep, especially during certain stages of sleep, the brain starts moving information from one part of the brain to the other. It's strengthening the connections between brain cells where memories are stored. But before we examine this phenomenon in a way that will help us learn faster, let's do a quick overview of the various stages of sleep so that we can grasp and understand this process a little better.

Stages of Sleep

Did you realize that all sleep is not alike? In fact, we go through various stages of sleep every night which provide different benefits to the body and particularly the brain. In her book, *Take a Nap! Change your life.*, Dr. Sara Mednick clearly describes and categorizes these various stages of sleep which we'll summarize here:

Stage 1:   The beginning stage of sleep when you're drifting from the structured thought of wakefulness into a loosening of mental associations. This is the least understood stage of sleep and is often referred to as the hypnogogic state. It's a kind of moving beyond our linear thinking and into free associations, also known as sleep-onset dreaming.

Stage 2: After about two to five minutes in Stage 1, your body temperature drops, and your heart rate slows. You have now slipped into Stage 2 and unconsciousness. Areas of your brain such as the brain stem and the prefrontal cortex slow down and literally "take a rest." Meanwhile electrical signals known as spindles, or lightning-quick oscillations, begin occurring. These electrical signals are nerve cells communicating with each other through chemicals called neurotransmitters. This stage typically lasts about 20 minutes., although we return to this stage several times a night before we enter a new stage of sleep, and we spend over 50% of our sleep time in this stage.

Stages 3 & 4:   As you cross into Stage 3 sleep you are entering a world known as slow-wave sleep (SWS). In this stage the stress hormone, cortisol, is completely shut off and you are getting extra growth hormone from the pituitary gland to fix the damages created by stress. Stage 4 may be considered as more of the same as Stage 3, except that this is now the very deepest stage of sleep, the slowing of physiological processes has continued even further.

REM: After briefly returning to Stage 2, we enter the

most fascinating stage of sleep known as REM, for Rapid Eye Movement. The heart rate speeds up, we take irregular gulps of air in contrast to the steady breathing of slow-wave sleep, blood pressure rises, and the blood vessels dilate. During this time a large amount of blood — 50% more than during your waking hours— flows to your brain and raises its temperature. Now the brain produces beta waves which are more characteristic of waking hours, and you experience vivid dreams. Because of the appearance of beta waves, the brain waves we produce while we're awake, this period has been called "paradoxical sleep."

This completes a full cycle of sleep: Stage 1, 2, 3, 4, and REM. Now, after a brief return to Stage 2, you continue to cycle through Stages 3, 4, and REM. If you are getting enough sleep, you will probably pass through the cycle four times.[20]

Benefits of Sleep Stages

The various stages of sleep perform different tasks and create a variety of benefits for our bodies. For us, and our pursuit of faster learning, it's helpful to know how these sleep stages affect the brain in terms of learning, memorization, and mastery of skills. Let's consider what happens in these areas during the different sleep stages:

Stage 1: As we mentioned this seems to be the least understood stage of sleep. However, many artists and mystics revere this period as a time when the imagination is freed to find creative solutions to problems.[21] Thomas Edison valued and used this state extensively to come up with creative solutions for his inventions. He reportedly would cat-nap in a specific chair while holding steel balls in his hands. When he drifted off to sleep (stage 2), the steel balls would fall out of his hands hitting a metal plate below and waking the famous inventor. Many times, he would have the answer to his problem, and if not, he would start the stage 1 napping process all over.

Stage 2: This stage comprises the majority of our night's sleep and is believed to be vitally important in increasing our alertness. Those neurotransmitters that are firing away during this period of sleep are also creating pathways and reinforcing previous neural firings that greatly enhance the learning of motor skills such as dancing, typing, driving, etc.

Stages 3 & 4: This period of slow-wave-sleep is regarded as a kind of reconstruction period for your brain. It has been regarded as a kind of pruning time for the brain when responses and memories that are no longer necessary are dismantled. In effect this stage is for "clearing your mind," which at the same time makes it easier for new learning pathways to form. SWS is believed to greatly enhance declarative memory — those figures, facts, and knowledge you need to remember. This period is also a time for ridding yourself of stress and anxiety which is vitally important for easier learning.

REM: This is the most important stage for strengthening

higher learning functions — mastering complex learning, memory, and creativity. During this period, information is transferred from a kind of short-term "holding tank" to more permanent storage places within the brain. Truly this is the most memory-enhancing period of sleep. In fact, without it, no significant learning can occur.[22] You need REM for faster learning!

So you see, sleep is vitally important both before and after learning. We need to get it, and we need to get enough of it.

Now, what about getting even greater benefits from sleep? Let's talk about naps.

The Perfect Nap

As Sara Mednick so carefully defines and describes it, the perfect nap optimally takes place between 1:00 and 3:00 p.m., and lasts 90 minutes, which allows your body to cycle through all the sleep stages once, with all of the stages being optimally balanced as follows:

Stage 1: 5%
Stage 2: 60%
Stages 3 & 4 (SWS): 17.5%
REM: 17.5%

In this single cycle through all the stages of sleep, studies have shown that the perfect nap can produce as many benefits as a full-night's sleep. That is, in well-rested people, so don't be tempted to think you can give up sleep and just nap.[23]

But in reality, you may not have the luxury of the perfect nap — at least not every day. What you can do, with a little strategic planning, is to get in what has come to be known as the Power Nap.

The Power Nap

Even if you've determined you can't get in the perfect nap, you can still receive enormous benefits from what is called the "Power Nap," a term that was coined by sleep researcher James B. Maas. This is a short nap (no more than 20 minutes) that allows you to experience Stage 2 sleep without crossing into slow-wave-sleep, which can cause you to wake up feeling groggy and drowsy. With a good 17 minutes of Stage 2 sleep, you can increase your alertness and ability to concentrate, elevate your mood, and enhance learning and memory. I highly recommend it!

Key 5: Sleep greatly increases your ability to learn and retain new information.

Get enough sleep, take naps, and learn faster!

Chapter 4

The Relaxing Side of Learning

When I first began researching accelerated learning techniques over 30 years ago, I was struck by the fact that each one included some kind of relaxation as a key component to faster learning. Researchers at that time stressed the importance of eliminating stress and tension from the body before optimal learning can take place. Since then, researchers have gained even further insights into the importance of relaxing the body to improve focus and concentration. When tension and stress are released from your body, and when your body is in a centered and completely relaxed state, your mind is free to concentrate fully on what you want to learn, centering every single volt of your mental energy on the topic at hand.

The ideal state for optimal learning is a relaxed body along with a heightened mental state. We'll talk about procedures and techniques for achieving this, but before we do, let's consider stress itself, so that we can be very clear about why it's important to eliminate it for faster and easier learning.

Stress — the Enemy of Learning

It's become almost common knowledge these days that stress, prolonged anxiety, fear, and all the negative emotions in that category can pose a serious threat to our physical health. In fact, many researchers in energy medicine believe that negative emotions are at the root of all, or at least most of the body's physical ailments.

I was impressed with the effect of stress on the physical body in a dramatic way during a lecture I attended many years ago by Hans Selye. Dr. Selye was the first person to systematically study the effects of stress on the body. During the lecture, Dr. Selye flashed a picture on a large screen of a healthy and perfectly beautiful white rat, followed by a picture of the same white rat a few months later after being subjected to constant stress. I, along with the rest of the audience, gasped in horror at the hideous sight of that shriveled up rat! I've never doubted the monumental effect of stress since.

But stress can be and is equally detrimental to the process of learning. Too much stress can, in a sense, put a clamp on the brain and inhibit its ability to learn new information. The brain simply cannot function at its best with the clamp of too much stress on it. Consider this from the book, *Superlearning 2000*: "A classic study at Georgetown University found that piled up stress can affect even eight-year-olds, lowering IQ as much as ten points."[24]

But getting rid of or lessening stress is just the beginning. We want to go beyond that and get the body into a deeply relaxed state in order to create a heightened, more aware, and vastly more alert mental state. This deeply relaxed physical state is at the heart of every rapid learning method I have studied and truly is an essential component.

But rather than spend more time discussing why it is so important to eliminate stress and relax the body, let's just get to the business of <u>how</u> to relax and learn faster.

Trying to Relax

You may very likely have been aware all along of the negative effects of stress and tension, and probably have "tried to relax" in many situations. Typically, the "trying to relax" brought with it even more tension, which in turn created even more frustration. Why? Because relaxation isn't something you try to do, it's something you must <u>allow</u>.

The idea of <u>trying</u> to do something was pointed out clearly to me by Dr. Maxwell Maltz, author of the groundbreaking work, *Psycho-Cybernetics*, at a lecture I attended many years ago in Denver. Dr. Maltz asked the audience members to "try to get up." A few people stood halfway up before Dr. Maltz cautioned, "NO, I didn't say 'Get up,' I said, 'Try to get up.' There's a big difference." Trying is do something is different from actually doing it.

I'm bringing up this point here, because many times in the past my students have said to me, "I've tried to relax, but I just can't!" We're not going to try to relax, we're going to look at exercises and techniques that enable the body to relax — there is a difference.

Take the Time

One more important point before we get to the exercises — you've got to allow yourself the time it takes to actively pursue a course of relaxation. It's strangely paradoxical but often true that during the times we most <u>need</u> to relax, to let go and unwind, we resist it the most. Students frequently used to say to me, "I just can't relax because I have all this stress." They also made statements like, "Sure, relaxation would be great but who has time for it?"

I'm not one to point any fingers here, however. I've been there myself. Most notably I remember a time when I was creating and delivering lectures for educational television. The pressure and stress of preparing three-hour lectures each week and appearing on live television mounted to the point where I was the proverbial nervous wreck. The director of the video network observed my increasingly anxious state and suggested I do some relaxation or meditation exercises. I actually heard myself say, "I would if I had the time!" This, after all my years of researching accelerated learning techniques and knowing the absolute necessity for relaxation! I'd given lecture/demonstrations on relaxation techniques, spoken on the subject at various conventions, and often conducted relaxation segments for students in my classes. My point is, the times when we really need to relax are often when we resist it the most.

But if we are to create that state in which we our ability to focus and concentrate is at its optimal level, we simply must take the time to get rid of the tension and stress and into a relaxed physical state.

Abraham Lincoln is often attributed with the following quote: "If I had eight hours to cut down a tree, I'd spend six hours sharpening my ax." That's what we're doing here — sharpening your ax — getting the body into a relaxed state with a heightened sense of mental alertness, prepared for easier and faster learning.

Relaxation Techniques for Faster Learning

As we've mentioned, trying to relax head-on rarely works. But a variety of relaxation techniques have all proven to be highly effective in allowing the body to let go of tension and stress and settle into a physical state that is highly conducive to learning. We'll describe several of the most popular and effective of these techniques and I encourage you to try all of them. You will more than likely find one or two that work better and more quickly than others in helping you get into that ideal physical state for learning. The important thing is to find what works best for you and to use it. Make relaxation an important and persistent part of your study routine.

Breathing

Perhaps the easiest relaxation technique, and one that you can use anywhere at any time without drawing attention to yourself, is the simple act of deep breathing. You can do the following breathing exercises while standing in line, riding the bus, walking between classes, or even while you're studying.

> **Exercise #1:** The most effortless relaxation exercise is to breathe in deeply from the diaphragm in long, slow, continuous breaths. Have the image of pulling the air in through your nose by expanding your abdomen until the lungs are completely filled with air. Hold for a moment, then allow the air to release slowly out through your slightly parted lips. This is so easy and yet it can have wonderful effects.

> **Exercise #2:** You can further the feeling of relaxation in the previous exercise by mentally saying to yourself phrases like, "I'm breathing in relaxation" as you breath in, and "I'm breathing out tension" as you breathe out. Or, use a mental image as you breathe such as visualizing the incoming breath as absorbing

all the tension, and the outgoing breath as carrying away the tension.

You can also think of more personal and imaginative phrases and imagery that have particular meaning and effectiveness for you. More structured breathing exercises can enhance the relaxation process even further. The following is a great exercise, but it requires privacy — unless you're completely uninhibited, in which case you can feel free to do it anywhere.

Exercise #3: Do the deep breathing exercises as described above but breathe out with a deep sigh. Voicing the sigh, as if you're experiencing great relief seems to intensify the effectiveness of the deep breathing.

Exercise #4: Breathe in slowly (using the diaphragm as previously described) to the count of 6, hold the breath for another count of 6, and breathe out to the count of 6. Be sure you are counting slowly! This works to significantly slow down and sustain the breathing process, enhancing the effectiveness of the entire deep breathing procedure.

You'll find that after only a few moments of doing any of these deep breathing exercises, you'll experience a noticeable feeling of relaxation. Practicing deep breathing regularly can lead to even deeper relaxation in which your mind is less encumbered with the tightness of stress and worry. That's exactly the state you want to achieve to allow you to learn easier and faster!!

Athletes and Relaxation

When I first began my research into accelerated learning techniques and realized they all required the prelude of a deeply relaxed body, I became fascinated with the fact that athletes seemed to be way ahead in their understanding of the importance of relaxation. In my search to find out how athletes achieved the heightened states of relaxation I contacted Dr. Jerry May, who at the time was Professor of Psychiatry at the University of Nevada - Reno and was the Sport Psychologist and a member of the Sports Medicine Team with the U.S. Alpine Ski team. In our conversation, Dr. May described to me how the competitor must be able to relax quickly in a pressure situation. In order to do this, Dr. May puts the athletes through extensive training exercises in deep relaxation and mental imagery. I thought it was interesting when he told me that in our society, most people feel they are relaxed when in reality they are just a little less tense. The condition of being deeply relaxed with the mind in a heightened state of alertness is a feeling many of us seldom achieve. But with training and continued practice, anyone can master it.

Progressive Relaxation

Dr. May and many other professionals recommend the use of a system known as Progressive Muscle Relaxation (PMR), a form of deep muscle relaxation, as the most effective way of training the body to let go of tension and its inhibiting restraints. The technique was developed by Dr. Edmund Jacobson and dates back to the early 1930's. It's a form of active relaxation as opposed to the kind of passive relaxation we'll discuss later. The purpose of progressive muscle relaxation is to relax the body by consciously tensing a muscle or groups of muscles, sustaining the feeling of tension for as long as 10 seconds, followed by relaxing those muscles with a deep sense of release and letting go for a period of about 20 seconds. The benefits of this type of relaxation are intensified when one focuses and concentrates on the muscle or muscle groups during the tension and release period and imagines a deep sense of all anxiety and tension leaving the body during the process.

The following is an example of this type of procedure:

Progressive Muscle Relaxation Exercise:

Find a comfortable position either standing, sitting, or lying down — most people find lying down works best. Close your eyes and breathe in deeply, holding the breath for a few seconds before releasing. After a few of these conscious, deep, sustained breaths, begin to relax into a passive attitude of letting go of any thoughts or concerns for outer circumstances and continue breathing slowly and gently.

Following this initial deep breathing and relaxation period, proceed by tensing all the muscles in one specific muscle group. Hold as tightly and intensely as you can and really focus on the tension for as long as 10 seconds or as long as you are able to hold it. Then release the tension with a great feeling of letting go, as if all the tension is escaping that particular area of the body like air being let out of a balloon. Relax and enjoy this feeling of deep relief for about 20 seconds before proceeding to the next muscle group.

Here is an example of a way to proceed through each of the muscle groups:

1. Forehead
2. Upper cheeks and nose.
3. Lower cheeks and jaws
4. Neck
5. Dominant hand and forearm
6. Dominant bicep
7. Opposite hand and forearm
8. Opposite bicep
9. Chest, shoulder, and upper back
10. Abdomen
11. Dominant thigh
12. Dominant calf
13. Dominant foot
14. Opposite thigh
15. Opposite calf
16. Opposite foot.

Many people have found it helpful to record a script of the tensing and relaxation process which allows them to relax into the procedure without having to think of the various muscle groups. An example of such a script might go something like this:

"I am now tensing all the muscles in my forehead — gathering every ounce of tension, squeezing it as tightly as possible. Every bit of stress and strain is compressed into this tensing of my forehead as I hold it and tense it increasingly. And now I release every bit of this tension from my forehead with a wonderful feeling of deeply letting go. I allow myself to relax in this wonderful feeling of welcome relaxation."

You can proceed in this matter with each of the muscle groups. By the way, the order of the muscle groups is not important. Experiment with what works best for you. Some people use a shortened version of this PMR exercise by combining the muscles into four large groups as follows:

1. Face and neck
2. Arms and hands
3. Chest, shoulder, back, and abdomen
4. Legs and feet

However you choose to proceed, you should practice the exercise every day until you can clearly distinguish the difference between when your body is tense and when it is relaxed. This awareness will help you consciously choose to relax, rather than allowing the tension to continue and increase. The more you practice, the deeper you will be able to relax and learn faster!

Relaxation with Mental Imagery

A modified type of Progressive Muscle Relaxation, one that is termed <u>passive relaxation</u>, can be especially powerful for individuals with a highly developed sense of imagery. Through mentally imaging the relaxation of muscles in various parts of the body, the same effect can be achieved as in PMR without the actual physical tensing and release. For me, this has proven to be especially effective and I encourage you to try it. Once again, it can be helpful to record a script for the mental imagery of relaxing the muscles for playback while doing the exercises.

Here is an example:

Mental Imagery Relaxation Exercise:

Find a comfortable position. Lie on your back or relax in a sitting position with your back supported. Close your eyes and begin to breath in very deeply and exhale with a sense of letting go.

After a few moments of slow, deep breathing, imagine yourself in your favorite, ideal place of relaxation — this may be on the beach, by a little stream, sitting under a tree, or some place of your choosing that allows you to feel very safe and comfortable. Take a moment to feel as if you are actually in this place, rather than just thinking of it.

As you sink into a very cozy, quiet, relaxed state of being, feel the warmth of the sun on the top of your head as it soothes and relaxes you, melting away any sense of tension that has accumulated there. Feel the soothing, relaxing warmth of the sun on your forehead as it eliminates any tension there. Continue to feel this relaxing sensation of the sun's rays as it moves over your eyelids and relaxes your eyelids and eyes. Feel the relaxing warmth of the sun as it eases the tension in your nose and cheeks. . . .

Continue in this manner, moving through each part of your body until you feel your entire body in a state of deep relaxation.

One note about this type of passive relaxation; if you find that you tend to go to sleep while doing the relaxation exercises (which, by the way, may be a sign that you need more sleep), sit on the floor against the wall or in a chair where your back will be supported. In other words, don't get too comfortable.

Relaxation with Mental Pictures

Another highly effective exercise utilizes mental pictures to evoke a relaxation response. This concept of relaxation with mental pictures is based upon the fact that the brain is unable to differentiate between an actual experience and one that is vividly imagined. The nervous system responds to images, especially those which are vivid and infused with meaningful emotion, as if the experience were happening in the moment and in the physical world. Because of that phenomenon, it's possible to get the same benefits of deep relaxation from mental pictures as you did from actually doing the relaxation exercises.

Let's look at a few possible scenarios for this kind of relaxation. The exercises below I have adapted from Dr. Maltz's classic book, *PsychoCybernetics*:

Relaxation with Mental Pictures Exercise:

Sit down in a comfortable chair or lie down on your back. Consciously focus on relaxing or "letting go" of any tension in the various muscle groups. Allow your forehead to relax, then your jaw, hands, arms shoulders, and legs. Spend about five minutes on this, which will be the extent of your conscious control of your body. Following this, you will bring to mind pictures that will automatically create the relaxation response.

Mental Picture No. 1

See yourself stretched out lying on your bed. Visualize your legs as if they were made of concrete. See the very heavy weight of these concrete legs causing them to sink way down into the mattress. Similarly see your arms and hands as if they were made of concrete. Again, the heaviness of the concrete causes your arms and legs to sink far down into the mattress. If you like, see a friend trying to lift your feet but finding that they are way too heavy to lift. Repeat this procedure with your neck, shoulders, and other parts of your body.

Mental Picture No. 2

You picture your body as a full-size marionette doll, with your hands tied loosely to your wrists with strings. Your forearm is loosely connected by a string to your upper arm, and your upper arm is connected loosely by a string to your shoulder. In a similar fashion your feet, calves and thighs are all connected loosely together with just a string. Your neck is just one limp string and the strings controlling your jaw are so loose that your chin is resting loosely on your chest. Finish with all the strings connecting the various parts of your body becoming so loose and lax that your body lies limp across the bed.

Mental Picture No. 3

In this scene your body consists entirely of inflated rubber balloons. You open a valve in each of your feet and the air starts to slowly escape from the balloons that are your legs. As the air continues to escape your legs slowly collapse on the bed and exist as deflated balloons. Similarly, a valve opens in your chest and the air from the balloons escapes, slowing deflating your entire chest as it limply collapses on the bed. Continue in this picturing with each part of your body.[25]

Dr. Malz suggests practicing these mental relaxation exercises for at least 30 minutes daily.

I have found that picturing beautiful, relaxing, pleasurable scenes which are not even associated with the physical body can be even more effective in evoking feelings of relaxation and well-being. By placing myself in situations which I find particularly pleasurable, and vividly imagining the sights, sounds and even physical movements that I would experience if I were actually in these scenes, I can within minutes move into a deep state of relaxation. Here are a few examples of these types of mental scenes:

Scene 1

You are floating on a raft down a peaceful, quiet, gentle river. You bask in the warmth of the sun and the gentle rolling of the raft as the waves come up under it. You hear the quiet, gurgling of the water which lulls you into a sense of deep tranquility.

Scene 2

You are relaxing in a hammock under a warm sun with a light breeze blowing across your face. You feel yourself swaying slowly and gently in the comfy hammock and lazily listen to the sweet chirping of nearby birds in the trees.

Scene 3

You are curled up in a big, overstuffed chair, or on a fluffy, soft rug in front of a warm fireplace. You feel the warmth from the fire and are comforted by its gentle crackling. You feel safe and very secure.

Scene 4

You are twirling around in a huge field of beautiful, abundant wildflowers. You smell their intoxicating scent and feel the brushing of their leaves and blooms against your legs as you dance in a carefree, joyful feeling of abandonment.

Scene 5

You are walking barefoot on a warm sandy beach, breathing in the salt air, and listening to the pounding surf. The warmth of the sun is magnificent, and you feel as free as the seagulls flying around you.

Scene 6

You are floating ever so gently on a huge, white, puffy cloud. You feel as if you are drifting along on a bed of cotton, and you are light as a feather as the gentle breeze carries you along.

I've described these scenes very briefly, but staying in them for a length of time is important to truly get their full benefit. Create scenes that are meaningful to you personally, based on your background and experience. For instance, if you have a fear of water, the beach will not hold great relaxing possibilities for you. On the other hand, if your most joyful and happy memories as a child were those of rollicking through the sand and surf with your family during those carefree childhood days, this type of image can easily return you to a time when stress and tension were far from your daily experience. Similarly, if you have a fear of heights, the common relaxation image of floating on a cloud could send you into a panic! You get the idea.

As you experiment with this technique, you will undoubtedly come up with scenes and situations that are even more vivid and appealing to you. Further, the images you choose will represent the dominant areas through which you process information. For instance, some people experience imaging better through sight, others through hearing, others through movement. Whichever sense mode you prefer, endeavor to make the images in your relaxation scenes as vivid and as real as possible. The fact that the brain is unable to differentiate between an actual experience and one that is vividly imagined, is the key factor in allowing you to achieve deep relaxation without actually being in any of the situations you are envisioning. Neat, huh?!

O━━▅ Key 6: Relieving stress is a key component to optimal learning.

Actively pursue and practice relaxation exercises to learn faster!

Put the Problem Aside

Have you ever worked and slugged away at something and the harder you tried the worse it got — only to discover after you gave up that it somehow clicked? This used to completely baffle me in my younger years when practicing some particularly difficult piano passage that seemingly got worse the more I practiced it. In complete frustration, I'd give up and go on to something else. Days later, deciding to tackle the dreaded passage again, I would often find that I could play it! I never quite understood it at the time, but I was always relieved and grateful. Years later I found Barry Green describing this phenomenon in his intriguing book, *The Inner Game of Music*: "When you can return to a calm and relaxed state, you may find that your unresolved problems have a way of receiving unsolicited solutions—without all that mental anguish."[26]

Arthur Koestler in his epoch classic, *The Art of Creation*, describes this time of putting the problem aside as the "period of incubation."[27] It is a time in which our unconscious continues to work on problems even when our conscious minds are occupied with other things.[28] One reason this period is so important to the creative process is that it liberates the mind from the restraints of the overly critical, inhibiting, logical left brain.

So, when you hit a "kink" in your studies and your efforts seem to be leading to only frustration and tension, put the problem aside for a day or two, or even a week if that's possible. Allow yourself this "period of incubation" and you might just be surprised by the new perspective you've gained when you return to the problem.

Take Regular Breaks

Just as we know that fatigue and stress interfere with your brain functioning, we also know that taking regular breaks during study improves your mental capabilities. It has been estimated that taking a 10-minute break after every 30 minutes of study can greatly improve mental effectiveness. The problem is in disciplining ourselves to be certain the 10minute break doesn't become a 15, 30, or even 45-minute break. I'm sure you know what I mean.

An ideal way to "break" is to get in 10-minutes of exercise. Take a walk around the block, run in place, do a few push-ups, stretch, bend, and breathe deeply. We've already discussed the fact that exercise is a great stress reliever, and the increased oxygen to the brain may be just the boost you need.

Taking in Further

Dr. Herbert Benson of the Harvard Medical School and the author of the ground-breaking book, *The Relaxation Response*, has put forth a fascinating new insight into the power of putting the problem aside which he describes as "The Breakout Principle." He states that after a hard mental or physical struggle, one needs to pull "the Breakout trigger" which he describes as follows:

> This event, which directly follows the struggle, has been variously described as 'letting go,' 'backing off,' or 'releasing' your mind from the hard-work mode. The most important characteristic of this second stage is that pulling the Breakout trigger *must completely sever prior thought and emotional patterns.* Our research has demonstrated that characteristic biological and molecular responses occur when the trigger is pulled.[29]

So how does one pull this so-called Breakout trigger? Dr. Benson suggests exercise, naturally, but also such things as taking a long shower, soaking in a bathtub, sitting quietly in a tranquil space, and listening to your favorite music. I'm assuming he's advocating things that you find pleasing, comforting, and obviously relaxing.

Dr. Benson also indicates that following this Breakout period, we can expect to experience creative insights, new ideas, and higher levels of performance. He believes there may be an actual scientific explanation for this. He suggests that this letting go of the problem may cause the brain to release large amounts of nitric oxide (NO) throughout the body which counters the effects of stress hormones. There we go again — letting go of stress! Try these ideas — they work!

⊙━━ Key 7: Letting go or backing off from a problem, can result in new ideas and higher levels of learning performance.

When faced with a difficulty, remember to "Put the Problem Aside" for a time, take regular breaks, and learn faster!

⊙━━

Chapter 5

The Musical Side of Learning

Having spent nearly my entire life in music, I am still in awe of the powerful mystique of music. The way it can dramatically and rapidly uplift and change our moods, bring us to tears, and evoke memories that have long been buried. Many people are convinced that relaxing to music can release emotional blocks which leads to enhanced creativity. Walt Disney, for example, had the soft sounds of Segovia's guitar music piped into the room as his animators and creators were working. And many other artists have found soft background music to be conducive to the creative process.

So it was with great fascination that I approached the research of those who pioneered the wave of accelerated learning techniques claiming that music could be used as a vehicle to create a psycho-physical state that enhances the learning process. These researchers believed that music could be used as a kind of bridge to calming the body, and allowing the mind to reach its greatest potential. This is an entirely different concept from listening to music for enjoyment. This is using music as a tool for heightened brain functioning. Let's examine how this works.

Music and Superlearning

The phenomenon of "Superlearning," brought about by the internationally best-selling book of the same title, fascinated educators (including me) across the country in the early 1980's. The authors, Sheila Ostrander and Lynn Schroeder, described how new techniques were proving that the learning process could be greatly accelerated and in fact, that the capacities of the mind were virtually limitless. One of these modes of learning, known as Suggestopedia, was developed by Georgi Lozanov, a Belgian doctor and psychiatrist, who asserted that when the body and left and right-brain thinking abilities are working together, learning abilities are greatly enhanced. A key component in reaching this synchronization of mind of body was the use of music described as follows:

> To strengthen memory, Lozanov would use music. He would start with slow movements of classical Baroque music, music that has a steady beat about once per second, sixty beats per minute. Music rather than sleep or hypnosis would calm the body so the mind could begin to realize its waiting potentials."[30]

This Baroque music stipulated by Lozanov is from a

period of that began around 1600 and continued into the early 18th century. The most well-known of the Baroque composers was of course Johann Sebastian Bach. Other composers from this period are Handel (think of the famous work, *The Messiah*), Vivaldi, and Teleman. It's easy to see why Lozanov believed Baroque music to be the most effective in getting the body into the kind of deep relaxation that allows enhanced mental awareness, because it is highly organized, predictable, and harmonic. The basso continuo — a type of bass line — that is so characteristic of this music, can be likened to a slow, human pulse, which is particularly relaxing when the music is performed at a pace of 60 beats per second. Baroque music can induce a kind of psychophysical state in which the body is freed from the tension that interferes with learning process and leaves the mind alert and more easily able to concentrate.

Against the backdrop of this slow Baroque music, Lozanov repeated information to learners in four-second bits. These short, four-second "chunks" of information were interspersed with four-second periods of silence. With this type of procedure, claims were made that an entire semester's worth of information could be learned in only a few hours.

Without delving more deeply into this entire process of Suggestopedia, you may just want to experiment with the use of Baroque music as a way to create a calm learning state within yourself - a kind of relaxed, yet focused centeredness. Here is a listing of a few selections of Baroque music that I recommend for encouraging this

state of relaxed body and focused mind:
<u>Baroque Music Examples for Relaxation:</u>

Bach, J.S.
  "Air" *from* Suite No.3 in D major
  (This is sometimes referred to as "Air on the G String")

  "Largo" *from* Concerto No.5 in F minor for Harpsichord

Handel, G. F.
  "Air" *from* Suite No. 1 in F major (Water Music)

  "Sarabande" *from* Suite No. 4 in D minor

Telemann, G.
  "Largo" *from* Viola Concerto in G major

Vivaldi, A.
  "Largo" *from* Winter (The Four Seasons)

Of course, there are many other examples of Baroque music and I encourage you to find the ones that most appeal to you and you find the most relaxing. In selecting recordings of these Baroque pieces or any others, be certain to choose the ones that are recorded as close to 60 beats per minute as possible. In other words, the tempo that feels like the secondhand ticking on your clock. This is not just a matter of aesthetics. We're talking about the physiological component of the music — the tendency of the music's pulse to lower the actual human pulse. Remember we're not selecting this music for our listening pleasure. Rather, the music is being used as a device to induce a highly relaxed body with an expanded degree of mental concentration.

Key 8: Listening to slow Baroque music can be used to synchronize the mind and body in an ideal state of relaxed and focused awareness, which is the optimal state for learning.

Listen to slow Baroque music for several minutes a day while relaxing into a focused awareness and learn faster!

Learning and the Mozart Effect

In the early 1990's, a study indicating that listening to the music of Mozart could raise IQ scores was so overly hyped that mothers ran out to buy CDs of Mozart's music hoping to create baby geniuses, and music stores began selling out of Mozart recordings! The research that prompted this craze took place at the University of California - Irvine and showed that a group of undergraduate students scored eight to nine points higher on a spatial IQ test after listening to ten minutes of Mozart. Even though the results didn't last, they were so astounding that conclusions were drawn that listening to music did affect the brain. One of the researchers, Gordon Shaw, expressed it this way: "We suspect that complex music facilitates certain complex neuronal patterns involved in high brain activities like math and chess. By contrast, simple and repetitive music could have the opposite effect."[31]

Following the study, a number of public schools reported that students' attention and performance were improved when Mozart was played in the classroom as background music.[32] But why the music of Mozart? Clearly many classical composers offer complex music that would seem equally capable of stimulating neuronal patterns. Don Campbell in his book, *The Mozart Effect* attempts to answer the question by citing the findings of the French physician and researcher, Alfred Tomatis:

> ...he (Tomatis) has found, again and again, that regardless of a listener's tastes or previous exposure to the composer, the music of Mozart invariably calmed listeners, improved spatial perception, and allowed them to express themselves more clearly — communicating with both heart and mind. He found that Mozart indisputably achieved the best results and long-term reactions, whether in Tokyo, Cape Town, or Amazonia.[33]

Dr. Campbell further explains the rationale behind the effectiveness of Mozart's music:

> Clearly, the rhythms, melodies, and high frequencies of Mozart's music stimulate and charge the creative and motivational regions of the brain. But perhaps the key to his greatness is that it all sounds so pure and simple.[34]

I'm not sure all the claims regarding the power of Mozart's music to actually raise IQ levels are valid, but I do know that music can have an almost mystical and magical effect in lifting us up and out of destructive and negative thought patterns that can act like tourniquets around our brains, inhibiting all that genius ability which we're being told we all have. Certainly, much of the music of Mozart is calming and centering and absolutely capable of nudging us into the kind of alert, relaxed state that is the centerpiece of optimal learning.

If you'd like to try listening to Mozart and experiment with its effect on enhancing your own learning abilities, I've listed a few examples below.

<u>Music by Mozart:</u>

Sonata for Two Pianos in D Major (K. 448) (This is the Mozart selection that was used in the original Mozart research at the University of California - Irvine.)

Clarinet Concerto in A Major (K. 622) "Adagio" Piano Concerto No. 21 in C Major (K. 467) "Andante"

Serenade #13 in G Major (K. 525) "Romance *from* Eine Kleine Nachtmusik"

Beyond Bach and Mozart

Albert Einstein is reported to have loved the music of Bach and Mozart the most. As we have seen, the music by these composers do appear to enhance our capabilities for learning. But what about other music and other composers? David Hamilton, in his delightful book, *It's the Thought That Counts*, provides some interesting insight into this question:

> It is not only Mozart that has such an effect, though. A 2007 study published in the journal *Behavioral Pharmacology* saw young adult mice exposed to slow rhythmic music for six hours a day for 21 days. While monitoring levels of a substance called brain-derived neurotrophic factor — a substance that aids the growth and survival of brain cells — the scientists found that it had increased in the hippocampus of their brains (the area that controls memory and learning). Thus, the brains of the mice showed a greater capacity for memory and learning, a finding that performance tests then supported.[35]

So there you have it — slow rhythmic music of any kind also seems to work. But did you catch the most exciting part of that quote — the bit about increased levels of brain-derived neurotrophic factor? That's the BDNF — that fertilizer, the Miracle Grow for the brain — the stuff that exercise produces! So here we see that listening to certain kinds of music has the potential to do the same thing! Fascinating!

Other Sounds of Music and Nature

I must tell you here that when I returned to the University following my first sabbatical leave to study accelerated learning, I was eager to experiment with the use of music in the classroom to enhance my students' learning and performance. I had carefully selected soft, slow, Baroque music at a pulse of approximately sixty beats per minute which I played in the background while I conducted the relaxation exercises I had created. Many of the students, as I had hoped, were excited and even exhilarated by the results of the exercises, feeling a dramatic release of tension and a better ability to concentrate. But a few students took me completely by surprise! Rather than allowing the steady, soothing strains of the music to relax their bodies and focus their minds, they were analyzing the music. Several of them waited for me after class with, "Was that recording by The Academy of St. Martin in the Fields?", "Could you tell me who the viola soloist was?", and "I thought that Largo movement was much slower than what I'm used to hearing." Clearly, they weren't getting the hang of it. To be fair, my students were all music majors and listening critically to music is what they were being taught to do.

Eventually, I started improvising, which is creating music in the moment, on the piano while conducting the relaxation exercises. I played slow, soothing music and watched a silent metronome light flash as I played to be certain I was keeping the music as close to 60 beats per second as possible. I experimented with several different types of improvisations but found that the ones I created in Dorian Mode seemed to work best. This is a type of musical scale arrangement that's similar to the common sound of major and minor, but has less feeling of structure. I was careful to create what I would describe as meandering melodies, with gently subtle and repetitive rhythmic patterns. It worked! My music students were able to stop focusing on the music itself with their left-brain analysis and settle into the relaxed state of focused awareness.

Eventually, I started experimenting with the sounds of nature as the "musical" tool do bring about that same state of relaxation and focused concentration. I found the "music" of waterfalls, gentle rain showers, a crackling fire, and perhaps best of all, the sounds of the seashore, could bring about deep relaxation while circumventing the analytical left-brain thinking activity.

I encourage you to experiment with what works best for you. Find the music or the sounds that most relax you, and which help to create a centeredness that allows you to more easily concentrate and focus. Be honest with yourself in doing this. If you're just playing your favorite tunes, or if you find yourself tapping or singing along to the music, you're off the track!

O━━ Key 9: Listening to Mozart and other slow music can increase the brain's ability to learn.

Listen to Mozart, or some type of slow, relaxing music, or even the soothing sounds of nature every day and learn faster!

Chapter 6

The Playful Side of Learning

At last, we get to the fun part — "The Playful Side of Learning," but it's also potentially the most powerful part of accelerating learning. We're talking about imagery or engaging the imagination to supercharge your ability to learn more effectively and faster. It's the action of imaging that makes the information yours — that gets it off the page and into your realm of knowing. In fact, this use of the imagination can be regarded as the "Magic Key to Faster Learning!"

So how does this work? Remember that right-brain hemisphere we discussed in Section 1 — the part of the brain that processes information through pictures, feelings, and images? When we engage that right-brain hemisphere along with the left-brain logical process of thinking, we enact a whole-brain mode of learning that makes learning faster and easier than you ever thought possible.

I'm convinced all the great thinkers throughout history not only knew of the power of imagination, or imagery, but utilized it in highly effective and powerful ways. Napoleon stated, "Imagination rules the world." And Einstein said, "Imagination is more important than knowledge." Both statements testify to the great power in the use of imagination.

We're going to apply this power of imagination to the learning process in fun and fascinating ways that I promise you — especially if you've never used it before — will astound you in its effectiveness!

Imagery

What exactly is imagery? In short, we can say it is seeing or experiencing within the mind. You did lots of this as a child when your imagination was operating freely, and creativity was a normal process of every day. Remember when you and your friends would shout, "Let's play like . . ., Let's pretend that . . ., You be _____ and I'll be _____?" It was easy. It was natural and fun. Sadly, our ability to create images in the mind many times atrophies somewhat as we get older. It doesn't have to, but here we get back again to our society's emphasis on left-brain logic. Gradually we begin to believe that the visualizing activities of the right-brain are not important — certainly not to the learning process.

But before we explore the fascinating ways of using

imaging to learn easier and faster, let's check out your imaging ability. We want to make sure your ability to image, or engage the use of your imagination, is geared up and ready to be put into action. The following sections contain exercises which will allow you to test your imaging power, experiment with it, and to practice strengthening it if need be.

How Vividly Do You Image?

Let's experiment with a couple of imaging techniques to give yourself an idea of how easily and effectively you can bring mental pictures to mind. One thing to keep in mind is that imaging is much easier when your body is relaxed, and your mind is free from struggle and strain. If possible, attempt these techniques at a time when you can be very relaxed, at ease, and centered.

Recall Imaging: These exercises, aptly referred to as "Recall Imaging" encourage you to bring to mind pictures of familiar places and events. I think it's an easy and effective way to start engaging the imaging process.

Recall Imaging Exercises: Get into a relaxed and comfortable position. Play some soft music if you find that soothing, close your eyes, and breathe deeply.

Exercise #1:

In your mind, travel to your apartment, house, or dormitory room — wherever you are living at the present.

If you are already there, place yourself in another room or part of your home. Notice the color of the walls, the arrangement of the furniture, the rugs on the floor, any artwork, or favorite items you have collected — picturing all of this in as much detail as possible. Feel as if you are actually there, rather than just thinking about it. Spend as much time here as you feel comfortable.

Exercise #2:

Again, with your eyes closed and in a very relaxed and easy manner, go back to the house or apartment in which you grew up. Walk through the rooms as you did when you were a child. Walk into the living room and sit down in one of the chairs. Walk into the kitchen and see the food you liked on the table. Go into your bedroom and enjoy seeing, even picking up, some of your favorite things that meant so much to you as a child.

Exercise #3:

In your mind's eye, return to a favorite holiday on which you were very happy and had a particularly wonderful time. Be there with the people who were with you. Again, taste the delicious food if that was part of it. Here the sounds of laughter or conversation. In other words, live the entire event again as if it were happening now.

If these exercises were easy for you, and you could readily image everything in vivid and vibrant detail, you're well on your way to putting that special power to use for rapidly accelerating learning. If you had some trouble or even a lot of difficulty with this, I encourage you to work with the following exercises that are designed to sharpen your imaging capabilities. If you take a little time and keep practicing, this ability to image will dramatically improve. As with anything, practice produces results. So, let's stay with it, so that you can use imaging to greatly enhance your learning.

More Than Seeing

If you felt like you were straining to "see" things in the previous exercises, it may help you to know that imaging not only applies to sight, but encompasses all the senses including hearing, taste, touch, and smell. A person can even have an inner sense of something without it being defined in terms of the physical senses. Since words and language are functions of the left-brain hemisphere, the right brain, which is nonverbal, may have an image which is difficult to describe. Be comfortable in knowing that whatever kind of imaging you're doing is valid, and don't worry if the images are less of a picture, and more of just a sense of inner awareness. Let's keep practicing.

Imaging With the Senses

Strengthening your imaging abilities will make this unique power even more effective when we start applying it to ways of learning faster and easier. The next set of exercises are designed to heighten your inner sense of sight, hearing, and taste, and may be a little more difficult than the previous exercises in which you were calling images to mind from the past, because in these exercises you are creating the images.

Imaging Workout Exercises: After you have read each of the following exercises, get into a comfortable position, close your eyes, and allow yourself to image the scenes with a feeling of ease. Remember not to strain or struggle with the imaging. If possible, have a friend read the exercises to you while you relax with eyes closed. Or you could record the exercises and play them back as you image so that you don't have to remember each detail. Above all, approach these exercises with a sense of fun and see what happens.

Exercise #1 for Sense of Sight:

In your mind, see standing in front of you a favorite female friend. She has as very beautiful smile, cascading dark hair, and is dressed in a long dark-purple dress with threads of glistening silver throughout. (Pause while you bring all of this to mind. Continue when the image is clear or as clear as possible.)

Now blink your eyes (in your mind) and see the dress change to red with gigantic white polka dots and your friend wearing a red bow on top of her head. (Pause)

Now see the dress changed to all white with twinkling lights. (Pause)

Finally, see your friend in an orange clown costume

with a big red ball in place of her nose!

Exercise #2 for Sense of Hearing:

In your mind, seat yourself in a comfortable position in your home with your phone at hand. Hear the phone ring and hear yourself answer it as you normally would. Clearly hear the voice of one of your relatives calling to ask how you are. Carry on a very pleasant conversation and hear all of it in your mind. Finish by saying "Goodbye." (Pause)

Hear the phone ring again and this time as you answer, you hear the voice of your best friend telling you that you have just won a car in a drawing. Enjoy the entire conversation. (Pause)

Hear another phone ringing with your favorite Disney tune. As you answer it, you're surprised to hear the voice of Mickey Mouse asking when you're going to visit Disneyland. Make plans for the two of you to get together and have fun. (Pause)

Here another phone ringing very softly — almost inaudibly. As you pick it up, you hear the tiny voice of the tooth fairy who apologizes for having the wrong number! (Pause)

Exercise #3 for Sense of Taste:

Imagine being blindfolded and seated at a table. You are presented with several different food items to taste. You smell the aroma of hot chicken soup, and as you lift the spoon to your mouth you spit it out because it is too hot. Quickly you drink a class of cold, refreshing water. (Pause)

You pick up a round piece of candy, and as you bite into it, you realize it is a chocolate-covered cherry. As you chew, you enjoy the rich chocolate taste, the juicy cherry, and the sweet, thick filling.

(Pause)

Now pick up a wedge of fruit. As you bite into it, you realize it is a sour lemon. Your lips pucker and your eyes close tightly. (Pause)

The last item you put into your mouth you realize isn't food, but an ice cube. You roll it around to keep it from freezing your mouth and either spit it out, or let it melt in your mouth.

How did you do with those exercises? Could you experience each one of them vividly? If it was difficult for you, don't worry. The more we work with imaging, the easier it will become and the more natural it will feel.

Stretching the Imagination

Let's take this process of imaging even further. The previous exercises, although admittedly tinged with some rather bizarre elements, are still primarily based on everyday possibilities — except perhaps for Mickey Mouse and the tooth fairy! But the biggest workout for the imaging process occurs when we create of images which are in the realm of the absurd and the preposterous. Why would we want to do this? Because the type of imaging which enables us to more easily learn and retain new information is that which creates a strong, vivid impression on the brain. We'll discuss this more in depth later, but for now, let's just have some fun!

The following set of exercises are designed to stretch your imaging ability beyond the normal. We're also testing your ability to truly silence the critical, analytical thinking of the left brain as you delve delightfully into the limitless world of right-brain creativity. Remember to keep your sense of humor and approach this with an attitude of fun.

Imagination Stretches: As with the previous exercises, find a comfortable place to relax, shut out the world, and enter the world of pure imagination. The brief statements are meant to be mere introductions for you to create your own vivid inner movies. Read one exercise statement, then close your eyes and allow at least a few minutes to vividly develop and play the scene in your mind. See how far you can go with this.

Imagination Exercise #1

1. A group of pigs playing football.
2. A giraffe riding a bicycle.
3. Chickens roller-skating.
4. Two spiders playing checkers.
5. An ostrich driving a car.
6. Two turtles playing hopscotch.

You may have been able to imagine all those scenes easily and effortless, in which case, you have a well-functioning, creative right-brain imagination. Or, you might have regarded them as too ridiculous to even bother with. In that case, we have some work to do. Let's try one more set — stretching the imagination to envision inanimate objects coming to life.

See if you can not only see but hear the following conversations.

Imagination Exercise #2

1. A refrigerator discussing a recipe with the stove.

2. Two living room chairs lamenting their fading colors.

3. A baseball and a baseball glove gossiping about the snooty bat.

4. A high-heel and an athletic shoe arguing about which of them gets treated worse.

5. A daisy flirting with a red rose.

6. A pencil and a pen comparing notes.

7. A pumpkin asking an apple how to lose weight.

Could you see it? Could you hear it? Wherever you are in your ability to image, the more you practice, the easier and more vivid this process will become. Perhaps you will be more excited about working with the idea of imaging if you can see how this process is applied to learning faster.

If you haven't tried it or used it before, you're about to embark on an entirely new adventure.

Imaging and Memory

So what <u>does</u> imaging have to do with faster learning? When it comes to memory — it has **everything** to do with it! The world-renown memory expert, Harry Lorayne, states emphatically that the secret of memory is that it's all done with association:

> "Anyone can learn to improve his or her memory. All we wish to remember must be associated in some way with something *we already* remember. Anything you remember now; you are associating in this way."[36]

He goes on to say that these associations are much easier to remember if they're made in a ridiculous, even illogical manner; "Each association must be illogical, and it *must be seen in the mind's eye.*"[37]

I'd like to tell you how I first became acquainted with this idea.

Storytelling

In my earliest research into techniques of faster learning, I attended the International Conference for The Society for Accelerated Learning and Teaching — yes, the SALT Conference! — in Ames, Iowa. On the first day, I sat eager and ready with pen and notebook in hand. However, I wasn't prepared for the presenter's opening statement, "I'd like you to write down the <u>names</u> of the planets in order of their proximity to the sun." I fidgeted with the pen and nervously tried to recall even the names of the planets, let alone their positions in the solar system! Thankfully I wasn't alone as others remarked that they couldn't do it. The presenter smiled, told us to put our paper and pens away, and invited us to sit back and listen to a story. It went like this:

It's a beautiful, warm, sunny day and you decide to sit and relax under a tree. However, your tranquility is suddenly disturbed by a loud rattling and clanging! You turn your head to the right and see an old 1965 **Mercury** car driving up the road toward you. As the car approaches, you see that it is being driven by the most beautiful naked lady with long, blond hair — she is **Venus**, the goddess of love and beauty. The car stops directly in front of you as a shouting woman runs up to the car dragging a large bag behind her. You recognize the woman as **Earth**a Kitt. She pulls a gigantic **Mars** candy bar out of her bag, then proceeds to get into the back seat of the car. No sooner is she seated, than the ground begins to shake and rumble and a ten-foot giant approaches. You're amazed to see that it is the king of the gods, **Jupiter**, as he climbs atop the hood of the car. As quickly as the car arrived, the entire group drives away exposing a three-foot wide license plate on the back which spells "SUN" — **Saturn, Uranus, Neptune**. A barking dog, **Pluto**, chases the car as it vanishes into the distance.

The presenter then asked us to take out our notebooks and write down the names of the planets, in order of their proximity to the sun. Seeing the story in my mind's eye, I easily and effortlessly wrote: Mercury, Venus, Earth, Mars, Jupiter, Saturn, Uranus, Neptune, Pluto. That was nearly 30 years ago, and I can still name the order of the planets in the solar system relying on this little story.

Now, this story is out of date and probably doesn't work for you at all. For one thing, you may not be familiar with Mercury cars as they are no longer being made. My first car was a Mercury so that one was a cinch for me. You may also have never heard of the exciting actress and singer, Eartha Kitt, as she is no longer living. I'm not even sure they make Mars candy bars anymore and I rarely see the Disney dog character, Pluto, these days. My point is this story was vivid and powerful for me as a memory device because all of it was relevant to me.

Your associations, your imaginings, must be vivid, relevant, and meaningful for you! As in life, don't use or live someone else's story!

Dual Coding

The story of the planets is an example of dual Coding — creating a picture (Right Brain) to enhance the memory of a word (Left Brain). Putting it all together we have the ultimate — "Whole-brain learning." You see, the idea is not to figure out how to get information into the brain, as there is ample evidence to support the fact that the brain stores everything.

The task is to figure out ways to register the information for greater recall. Associating the information through forming pictures is a powerful technique for registering the information in a way that you will be able to recall it later.

Dominic O'Brien describes how he discovered this effective technique in his early attempts to memorize a deck of 52 playing cards in sequence:

> I realized that to memorize a string of unconnected data, such as sequences of cards, involves first coding them into images. In this way, the pieces of unconnected information can somehow become connected together. I now know that that this process of using imagination brings into play a whole range of brain functions, including logic and spatial awareness.[38]

We also know that information is more easily remembered when it is unusual, or out of the ordinary. Think about this for a minute. You more than likely will not remember (be able to recall) many, if any of the events of a typical day several years ago when you got up at your usual time, went through the usual day's activities, and retired without anything unusual taking place. But undoubtedly you can, with a little effort, recall a Thanksgiving from three years ago — whom you were with, what you did, where you were. This day was out of the ordinary — unusual events took place. Creating unusual images is the most effective in impressing the brain.

The Von Restorff Effect

This idea that we can strengthen memory by presenting information in some outstanding way is known as the "von Restorff effect" after the researcher of the same name. Peter Russell describes this phenomenon in *The Brain Book*:

> Von Restorff found that three digit numbers were better learned if presented within a list of nonsense syllables than if surrounded by other numbers. . . . The effect has since been found to be true in any situation in which items stand out in some way from those around them or are in any way surprising. Thus, a brightly colored picture is better remembered than the black and white ones surrounding it, and the tall girl with husky voice will stick in your memory better than many other people.
>
> One possible explanation is that the outstanding elements increase a person's attention, which in turn leads to better memory.[39]

This concept is of course best proven through experience, and you can test the idea by converting any list of dry, dull facts into colorful, funny, unusual, or bizarre scenes. We'll be experimenting with this more as we go to work on specific examples.

Emotions in Learning

The infusion of strong emotions into the image intensifies the impressing of information on the brain in a way that will make it readily accessible. Once again, recalling an average day in the past is quite difficult for most of us, but the day we were embarrassed beyond belief, the time and place we met our first love, the day we lost someone very special to us — these days come to mind as easily as if they were yesterday. And don't forget, humor is associated with powerfully positive emotions and its use can be very effective in learning. Now I ask you, when was the last time you thought humor had anything to do with learning?!

Personalizing Information

If you want to really cinch your ability to recall information, personalize it in some way by placing yourself in the picture. Get involved in the words or the material you are endeavoring to commit to memory. Dominic O'brien thinks getting yourself involved in the story works so well because it attaches feeling and emotions to it.[40] Keep in mind that anything is possible in the imagination, so you can manipulate any scenario to involve yourself in absolutely any way you choose.

Let's examine a way to put all of this together.

Memorization Exercise:

Here is a list of Five State Capitals and their corresponding states:

1. Dover, Delaware
2. Frankfort, Kentucky
3. Augusta Maine
4. Lincoln, Nebraska
5. Olympia, Washington

Knowing what we know now about imaging and the use of the right brain in learning, we won't try to memorize this list by repeating it over and over, hoping it sticks. Instead, we'll make up some unusual, bizarre, and funny stories to impress the information on our brains. **And**, we'll put ourselves in the story —something like this:

Dover — Delaware: Your friends look at you aghast as you describe how you **Dove** off a 1,000-foot cliff in a state where all the girls are named **Dela** and **ware** only aprons.

Frankfort — Kentucky: You're laughing and shouting and having a wonderful time at the **Kentucky** Derby, while eating 100 **Frankforters** in a contest.

Augusta — Maine: It's **August** and you're celebrating the end of summer vacation with the whole town on **Main** Street.

Lincoln — Nebraska: You and Abraham **Lincoln** are having a wonderful time cheering (for or against) the **Nebraska** Cornhusker football team.

Olympia — Washington: You are **Washing** a ton of

clothes, when an **Old** man with a **lymp** comes up and asks if he may assist you.

Okay, so we spelled a few words incorrectly to make the associations.

But you get the point.

Now you may be thinking that this could work fairly easily when attempting to memorize a list of names or words. But what about more complicated or more lengthy information?

More Advanced Memorization Exercise:

Let's assume you're required to memorize the complete list of Shakespeare's comedies. I'll arrange them as follows:

1. The Tempest
2. The Two Gentlemen of Verona
3. The Merry Wives of Windsor
4. Measure for Measure
5. The Comedy of Errors
6. Much Ado About Nothing
7. Love's Labours Lost
8. A Midsummer Night's Dream
9. Merchant of Venice
10. As You Like It
11. The Taming of the Shrew
12. All's Well That Ends Well
13. Twelfth Night
14. The Winter's Tale

This list can look quite daunting at first — unless you're a Shakespearean scholar, which let's assume you're not. So what do we do? We can tell ourselves a vivid, wild, crazy, and personal story. Read the following story slowly, pausing after the mention of each comedy to image the action taking place fully and clearly while committing each title to memory.

The Story of Shakespearean Comedies

You set sail in a small craft on the open sea when a tremendous storm comes up. Lightning is flashing, thunder is crashing, your boat rocks so high you're in danger of being capsized. It truly is **The Tempest**!

Mercifully **Two Gentlemen** on a huge ship named **Verona** come to your rescue.

The gentlemen take you aboard their ship where you are delighted to meet their wives, whom they laughingly introduce as **The Merry Wives of Windsor**.

But you are horrified at the sight of their grotesque children who run by you! They clearly **Measure Four** feet wide with a **Measure**.

You inquire as to why the children are so wide and everyone laughs and says it was just an error — truly **The Comedy of Errors**!

The laughing stops as everyone stares dumbfoundedly at a servant who approaches with a calculator exclaiming that he keeps doing much adding on the calculator but gets nothing — truly, **Much Ado About Nothing**.

However, you feel great compassion for the poor servant as one of the wives tells you about the man's **Love** for whom he **Laboured** tirelessly but was **Lost** at sea.

Weary of all this craziness, you retire to bed. It is very hot, **A Midsummer Night** as you begin to **Dream**.

In your dream you are carried away to Italy where you meet **The Merchant of Venice**.

The merchant is very friendly and offers to make you a gift of any of his wares, just **As You Like It.**

Your conversation, however, is interrupted by his wife who begins screaming hysterically upon hearing about the offer! You pity the poor merchant and think **The Taming of the Shrew** must be impossible!

Thankfully, you wake up from your nightmare and are relieved to find that it was just a dream. At least **All's Well That Ends Well**!

On the **Twelfth Night** you are rescued from sea and are elated to return home to your family. Years later, on a cold and snowy night, your grandchildren beg you to sit by the fire and tell them **The Winter's Tale**. You relive the entire experience for them of being rescued at sea — much to everyone's delight.

Now, see if you can write down all fourteen of Shakespeare's comedies. You will do this by replaying the weird tale in your mind and visualizing each event as it happened. As the name of each play occurs in the story, you will write it down. Depending on how well acquainted you are with these plays, you may be able to do this quite easily! If you are unable to write down all the plays, just go over the story again in an easy and relaxed manner, and really make the action and characters come to life! Image with all the senses as we discussed earlier. Really feel the boat rocking in the beginning of the story as the storm comes up. Smell the perfume of the Merry Wives. Hear the shrill voice of the Shrew! You get the idea.

Now notice I didn't say try harder — work harder — concentrate more — any of the usual berating things we often say to ourselves when we are unable to remember something. Because as we've learned, stress and strain only hinder your mental abilities. So let it be relaxed and fun. This is all about learning faster. And one of the main keys to learning faster is making it easy!!

Making Your Own Stories

The memory stories we've told so far have been of my creation, and for that reason may not be particularly effective for you. They were presented here merely to serve as examples. The stories you create for yourself, using your own associations, images, and references, will obviously be much more powerful. I think it's helpful to remember when you are making your associations, creating the images for greater recall, that you go with the first images that come to mind. Let this be easy and lighthearted. I believe it's a mistake to struggle and strain to create images that you think will have the most relevance. That's your left-brain logic interfering with what is meant to be the playfulness and spontaneity of the right brain.

It's also helpful to make you associations as personal as you can. You can do this by including people you know, places with which you are familiar, situations and scenes you know well. Also, keep in mind that the crazier the images, the more they will impress the mind, and the easier they will be to remember. Above all, have fun with the imaging. Many memory techniques are even referred to as games, which is not surprising when you realize that humor and a sense of play are a great asset to learning.

The more you practice imagery and making associations the easier it will become. And you can practice this easily almost anytime and anywhere — standing in line, while exercising, washing dishes, folding clothes, you name it. The more you work with this, you'll find images popping into your head that will have you laughing and wondering, "Where did that come from?"

Further Ways to Personalize

So far, our imaging techniques have only been applied to lists of words, names, and titles. But your ability to personalize information and tap into right-brain imaginative powers can be utilized in nearly every facet of learning. Let's take a situation in which you find yourself not wanting to study, or even resisting a subject matter altogether. In fact, you say you can't stand the subject and are no good at it. It stands to reason that if you're not interested in a subject, you're probably no good at it. Instead of fighting the situation, we can use our imaging faculty to help us out.

Assume you're required to study Shakespeare. I like this example because "Introduction to Shakespeare" was one of my favorite courses in college. But let's also assume you have no interest in Shakespeare. In fact, you say, "I hate Shakespeare! The guy lived 400 years ago. How the heck am I supposed to personalize information from someone like that?" Well for starters, keep in mind that nothing about the right-brain processes needs to be particularly logical and you can be and do anything in your mind.

Here we go.

You're having trouble getting into, so to speak, the plot of a Shakespearean play. You read from the position of a student living four centuries later who can't imagine having one thing in common with this guy and his "weird" sounding English. Quite naturally, you are reading and processing the information on a superficial level through a lack of involvement, "And it must follow as the night the day," **Thou canst not remember a thing**!

Enter right-brain imaging. We'll play "let's pretend" as we did as children. You are a brilliant New York actor auditioning for the role of one of the characters in the play you're studying. Securing this role means life or death to you career and you study the play as if your very life depended on it. Better yet, with a little more stretch of the imagination, you are one of the characters in the play — you feel as he or she feels, think as he or she thinks, and live the very life of the play.

Or perhaps you are Shakespeare's closest friend. He has entrusted you with this manuscript of his latest play and is eagerly awaiting your comments. After you've read the play, the two of you engage in lively conversation concerning the plot, motivation, development of the characters, whatever you like.

Or maybe even a bigger stretch — you are Shakespeare! You're reading the words you have personally written and understand more than your professor. However, I wouldn't mention that to your professor.

Playful? Yes. Fun? You can make it so. Idiotic? Not as much as you might think. Don't dismiss it until you've tried it. I think you will be quite surprised at how a little make-believe right-brain imaging can not only get you over the negative attitudes that are inhibiting your learning but can also get you into a deeper understanding of the subject you may have been resisting. Give it a try.

Super Memory

At this point, some of you may be thinking, "That imaging stuff is fine for all of you "artsy" types, but I'm studying chemistry, math, accounting, physics, etc., and none of those little pretend games and stories are going to help me with the numbers, facts, formulas, or principles that I need to learn. Believe it or not, <u>anything</u> can be transmuted into an image, thereby enhancing your ability to impress your brain for greater recall.

The story is told of Solomon-Veniaminovich Shereshevesky (would I make this name up?) who from all indications was able to remember everything from complex mathematical formulas to long lists of nonsense syllables — all of which he was able to recall fifteen and twenty years after he had originally committed them to memory. This Russian journalist was studied by the Russian neuropsychologist A. R. Luria for thirty years, during which time he discovered that Shereshevesky's extraordinary memory feats were accomplished through imagery and associations. Numbers, letters, symbols, foreign vocabulary words — anything — can all be imaged. Consider these possible imaging associations:

Diameter —. putting a dime in a meter

Ratio — "I'll race 'yo' to the corner!"

Pi — you're eating a pie — your favorite.

Circumference — you're having a great time at the circus in France.

Anything can be imaged! Listen to Dominic O'brien, the eight-time World Memory Champion, again as he describes this; "... I've shown that it's possible to memorize far more than nine digits (in fact, I've memorized well into the hundreds!) at a time, as long as you have a strategy for doing it."[41] He further states;

> Until I started to perform feats of memorization, sequences of numbers to me seemed unintelligible and instantly forgettable. However, now when I look at a series of numbers, they appear completely differently to me. They come to life; they are animated, colorful, and even at times humorous. Now, numbers have characters all their own. Why? Because I have developed a way to convert them from (to me at least) their normal, dull, meaningless form into something that my brain can work with. The secret to memorizing numbers is to attach significance to them by translating them into coded images.[42]

You see, anything can be associated with an image. As you work with this, let your imagination play. You'll find that techniques and ideas for imaging even complicated formulas can and will come to you. Remember to make your images meaningful and relevant to you, and they will be far more powerful than any that even the experts contrive for you.

Convince Yourself

The only way to truly understand the memory techniques we have been discussing is to try them for yourself and practice them in as many situations as possible. Discover for yourself that the entire learning process can be fun.

And what of the snobs who tell you that all of this is silliness and not befitting of the true intellectual? You may inform them that memory techniques were practiced extensively by the ancient Greeks and Romans and are utilized to a greater or lesser degree by everyone. The brain processes information through association. What you are doing is consciously magnifying or intensifying the associations to register the information in such a way that it can be easily recalled. Keep in mind that the brain stores everything. Your job is figuring out ways to retrieve the information or bring it back into your conscious mind whenever you need it.

Put you imaging faculty to work. Image vividly. Bring the information alive. Make the imagery ridiculous, exaggerated, humorous, and wildly out of the ordinary for the maximum effect. You'll be amazed!

O━━▄ Key 10: Associating new information with previous information through imaging greatly enhances the learning process.

Image new information vividly, clearly and even outrageously, and learn faster!

Self-Imaging

Perhaps even more powerful and more important than the use of imaging in the process of memory, is another

O━━▄

kind of imaging that can make all the difference in how easily and effectively we are able to learn. I'm speaking of self-imaging — the image we hold of ourselves. In Chapter II we discussed the power of beliefs on the learning process — how our own beliefs can be a tremendous asset or can essentially put a tourniquet around our brain's natural learning abilities. I asked you to take a short and simple quiz to assess how you think of yourself. Do you believe you are a fast learner, a slow learner, or something in between?

All of us have had times when we failed at something. But how we regarded those failures may be governing our learning abilities now more than we realize. The teacher criticizing a paper or a project, the parent lamenting that "you haven't got a brain in your head," even the so-called friend who made fun of something we tried to do that was very important to us — all have contributed to a mental picture we carry around of ourselves and our abilities. Unfortunately, that mental picture is often negative. It's not that we want this. It's not an idea of ourselves that we consciously created. But we've lived with it for so long that it feels natural, and we believe it's the truth about ourselves.

Dr. Maxwell Maltz in his unparalleled classic book on self-imaging, *Psychocybernetics*, describes this as being hypnotized by false beliefs. He states that the negative ideas we hold of ourselves are just as powerful as the ideas planted into the mind of a hypnotized subject by a professional hypnotist.[43] What we <u>believe</u> about our abilities to learn quickly and easily is governing those abilities.

But the exciting part of this is that we can change this image of ourselves. We can remove the negative beliefs. How? Once again, the Magic Key is Imaging!

As we've discussed, the subconscious is unable to determine the difference between an image that is real, as in actually taking place in the objective world, and one that is vividly imagined. You see where this is leading. We can CHANGE that image of ourselves through creating and vividly imagining what we wish to become. Let's talk more about how we can set out to do this.

Alpha Imaging

This new image of ourselves — a person who is able to learn quickly and easily and enjoys the entire learning process and even finds it fun -- is not going to pop up magically with a superficial change of thought. What we need to do, is convince the subconscious mind that our former belief, or view of ourselves, as a person of limited abilities is no longer valid. The subconscious must now understand that we are free to learn faster than ever before and that learning for us is easy.

The state of mind in which the subconscious is most susceptible to accepting this new picture of ourselves is something known as the alpha state. This is that kind of twilight state you experience just before you fall asleep, when you are carried away by a daydream, and that kind of dreamy state you experience just as you are waking up. It is more than just a feeling of being very peaceful and relaxed, it is a state in which the brain waves are functioning at about seven to fourteen cycles per second. In our normal waking state — known as the beta state — the frequency of our brain waves ranges from about fifteen to forty cycles per second. For that reason, just as you're falling asleep at night, and as you are waking up in the morning are the two best possible times to see yourself in your mind's eye, and to tell yourself — so that the subconscious can hear you — that you are now a person for whom learning is easy. Of course, it's possible, and many people have done it, to train yourself to enter the alpha state at any time during your waking day, but for starters, the going to sleep and waking up times are the very best opportunities for impressing your subconscious mind with a new self-image. Let's try this out.

<u>Exercise for Enhancing Learning by Changing the Self Image:</u>

Find a time and place where you can most influence your subconscious mind — either falling asleep, upon waking, or while sinking into a deeply relaxed physical and mental state. Bring to mind a learning situation which is very relevant and important to you. It could be a course you are taking, a physical skill you want very much to improve, or something you have always wanted to learn. As much as possible, place yourself IN the image — BE there, rather than just looking on as an observer. Sense the great satisfaction and joy as you experience how quickly and easily you are comprehending the information. You are amazed at how effortlessly you understand all the material and find that the recall is equally effortless. Engage in conversations with your friends who are patting you on the back for being such a whiz at this subject. Hear your relatives congratulate you on your learning abilities or ask you how in the world you can learn the material so fast! Take enough time to thoroughly bask in the delight of this experience.

After doing this exercise, see yourself — feel yourself — learning easily. Experience the joy of having mastered something that previously seemed difficult or even impossible for you. Carry around an idea of yourself as someone who can learn easily. Convince yourself that <u>nothing</u> can prevent you from learning anything. Some subjects may take you longer than others to assimilate, but nothing can prohibit you or stop you from mastering whatever you choose.

At first this is going to seem phony — perhaps even uncomfortable — and you'll probably say to yourself, "I'm just kidding myself." "I've always been a slow learner and just saying that I'm now a fast learner isn't going to make it so." But by repeating these and similar scenes over and over in your mind, the whole concept of learning faster will not only seem possible but will gradually become a reality for you.

As you get further and further into self-imaging

exercises, new ideas for visualizing will pop up and you will find yourself becoming more and more confident. Gradually, these feelings of self-confidence begin to feel normal — just as the negative feelings of inadequacy had previously felt normal. You will experience the great satisfaction of having changed yourself from within.

You need to do this consistently and repeatedly before any real change in your self-image can be created — but it does work. Practice self-imaging every day and refuse to give in to any negative beliefs about your learning abilities. Dr. Maltz states that it usually requires a minimum of 21 days to effect a perceptible change in one's mental image. So, if possible, reserve judgment about your ability to change your mental image for at least that length of time.[44]

This ability to impress the subconscious mind through imaging is so powerful that more and more people are discovering that it's possible to heal the body of many diseases using this technique. David R. Hamilton, who earned his Ph.D. in organic chemistry and worked as a scientist in the pharmaceutical industry, left his profession to study and write about how powerfully our thoughts and images affect our bodies. In his book, *How Your Mind Can Heal Your Body*, he cites case after case of people who have healed themselves through imaging. In fact, he states; "Visualization isn't just a subjective thing or an inert mishmash of mental pictures just there to make you feel good, but a process that causes real chemical and structural changes in the brain."[45]

Work with this powerful process of seeing yourself as someone who learns easily. It could very well turn out to be the most important and most powerful part of your transition to faster learning!

O━━ Key 11: Our beliefs about our learning abilities powerfully determine the ease with which we are able learn. Limiting beliefs can be changed by impressing the subconscious with new and more positive self-images.

Vividly and consistently picture yourself as a person who learns quickly and easily and learn faster!

Chapter 7

The Performance Side of Learning

In almost all learning situations, there comes a time when we are called upon to demonstrate what we have learned — to prove that we have mastered the material. I'm referring to this as the Performance Side of Learning because this proving that we are competent in an area usually takes the form of some kind of performance. Most commonly, in traditional learning situations, these demonstrations are in the form of a written test, or an oral presentation or speech. In athletic endeavors, it shows up as a competition or a game. In my world of music, it was the solo recital or concert.

Now, no matter how you have improved your ability to learn faster and more easily, an inability to perform well on an assessment of some type can blow the whole thing. Yikes!! We won't let this happen. We're going to examine ways to ensure that the performance side of learning takes place with optimal ease and effectiveness. Let's take the most obvious performance requirement — tests.

Taking Tests

It probably goes without saying that the greatest threat to one's ability to perform well on tests is anxiety. You fear that you haven't learned the material well enough (although I'm assuming you're over that now), or you fear that you will not be able to remember the information during the exam. This fear is amplified if it has indeed happened before and you're remembering in vivid detail how gloriously you bombed.

This crippling fear known as test anxiety can inhibit your ability to perform at your best. Dr. Bruce Lipton, a cell biologist and former Stanford Medical School professor addresses the debilitating effects of fear in his groundbreaking book, The *Biology of Belief*. He states quite bluntly, "The simple truth is, when you're frightened, you're dumber."[46] Now that's direct! He goes on to say; "Teachers see it all the time among students who 'don't test well.' Exam stress paralyzes these students who, with trembling hands, mark wrong answers because in their panic, they can't access cerebrally stored information they have carefully acquired all semester."[47]

So what do we do about it? We can tell ourselves not to get nervous, but I think most of us can attest to the fact that this rarely works. All the "trying not to get nervous" and lecturing yourself over and over, "relax, relax, relax" usually insures a state of increased tension. I'm sure many of you have felt the frustration of being told, "If you're well-prepared, you won't get nervous," which isn't true for the sufferers of test or performance anxiety.

Listen to how Timothy Gallwey describes his experiences with tennis students and "trying to relax" in his book, *The Inner Game of Tennis*.

> Now I've got the secret to this game; all I have to do is make myself relax.' But of course, the instant I try to make myself relax, true relaxation vanishes, and in its place is a strange phenomenon called 'trying to relax.' Relaxation happens only when *allowed*, never as a result of 'trying' or 'making.'[48]

We talked a little about this "trying to relax" in Chapter IV, but now we're discussing it as it directly applies to relaxation during test taking, or any other kind of performance. Certainly, the relaxation exercises you have done will help, as your overall stress levels are greatly reduced. But what brings up this anxiety when it's time to demonstrate or prove what we've spent so much time learning? Where is this fear coming from? Ah yes, the image — the imagination — the inner picture of yourself failing!

The Power of the Picture

"A picture is worth a thousand words." You've no doubt heard the expression. But in performance of any kind, picturing your desired outcome or result, concentrating on it without tension or trying to make it happen, feeling the happiness, satisfaction, and joy of great success, then allowing your subconscious mind to enact that picture, is a powerful way to success. The problem is, we often do this beautifully, but in the negative!! We see, feel, experience what we don't want to happen with great worry, fear, and dread, then wonder why we're so full of anxiety.

Here are some examples: You have the thought, "What if I can't remember the names, dates, facts, figures, etc.?" and a vivid inner picture accompanies those thoughts which generates the fear as if it were true. Other thoughts such as, "What if I can't think of a single word to write on the essay questions? What if my mind goes totally blank?!" generate more pictures and increasingly anxious feelings. It seems hopeless, right? Absolutely not! Those pictures can be changed and with deliberate, focused practice, you can create the kind of pictures that will generate confidence, and profoundly enhanced performances.

Changing Pictures

If the inner pictures of fear and failure have been with you for a long time, it's going to take some effort to create new, positive inner pictures of success and confidence, but believe me, it's well worth the effort. And best of all — it works!!

We explored relaxation exercises in Chapter IV, and

in Chapter VI we worked on imaging exercises to speed the learning process. We also combined relaxation and imaging into a self-imaging process to enhance our beliefs about our learning abilities. Now we're going to direct those two processes — relaxation and imaging — to changing the inner pictures from ones of anxiety and failure to those of confidence and success. The following exercise is designed to do just that. Let's get to work.

Exercise to Eliminate Performance Anxiety

Find your most comfortable place of relaxation, quiet, and solitude. The setting for this exercise is very important as your success depends upon the degree to which you are able to withdraw from the outer world and get into the inner space of your subconscious mind.

Bring to mind a situation, a circumstance, or a particular time in which you were very successful and experienced a wonderful feeling of self-confidence. (Please don't say you can't think of anything — there has to be at least one time — probably many more — when you felt really good about yourself, who you were, and what you were doing.) Take as long as you need to find and bring up the image of this time that resonates with you in a powerfully, positive way.

Now, relive those great feelings of pride and self-respect as vividly as possible. Feel all the positive emotions. Live in this happy, positive time again as if it were happening now.

When you have allowed yourself considerable time to

reaccess and relive these positive feelings (I recommend a minimum of ten minutes), keep those successful feelings very much alive within you, and bring to mind the test, essay, speech, sporting event, recital, or presentation that is facing you now. Superimpose this new image onto the image of the former successful time in your life that you have been reliving. Instead of trying to <u>make</u> yourself feel positive about the event that is confronting you, just bring the event into the world of your already positive feelings. If you've managed to conjure up and delve into the former positive feelings sufficiently, the new performance challenge can be allowed to take on the glow of success. Now, instead of dreading the exam or _____ (you fill in the blank), you can come into a positive and expectant feeling of success about it.

I recommend you do this many times. You could say it's a way of tricking the mind, but I prefer to think of it simply as changing the energy patterns you've allowed to surround your upcoming challenge. When you think of whatever it is you're facing, instead of the negative energy patterns of doubt and fear, you're supplying the positive energy of optimism and confidence. If you practice this enough, you will find when thinking of your upcoming performance event, the old images of failure will have been replaced by new images of success. And you know what they say — success breeds success. The more you can feel successful and self-confident, the more you will succeed, and the easier it will all become.

Making the Images Real

Now that you have replaced the former fear and failure patterns with positive and successful energy patterns, you can work directly with the task confronting you to make the imaging more real and believable to your subconscious mind. Here is an example:

The Test (Examination): With those successful feelings very much alive within you, place yourself mentally at the exam. If you are taking it in a classroom, sense the other students around you. Talk with them (mentally) in a relaxed way with a good feeling of knowing you are about to perform extremely well. See the teacher walking into the classroom carrying the stack of exam papers. Feel the wonderful, although perhaps different, sense of confidence and optimism as the exam is laid on your desk. And then, relax into an almost blissful feeling of marking each of the answers with ease — experience yourself knowing all the answers and marveling at how you are taking the test in such a calm and confident manner. Turn in the exam, leave the classroom, and say a private little "You did it!" to yourself. What a great feeling!

If your exam is taking place online or in another setting, you will of course modify the preceding scenario to reflect that venue, but the principle of living the exam in the moment, feeling confident and at ease, and completing it successfully remains the same. Here are some other possible variations:

Writing the Essay: As the Blue Book, or other writing

paper is placed on your desk, you calmly pick up your pen and are very much aware of how differently you feel from before — no more sweaty palms or churning stomach. You're confident that you've mastered the subject (of course you've studied — this won't work without the preparation) and you find yourself eager to express what you know. You find the pen almost gliding across the page and the material practically organizing itself as you write.

Now that's a good feeling!

Giving the Speech or Presentation: Your note cards are in hand, and you're enthusiastically looking forward to delivering the information which you've carefully prepared. You take a few long, deep, calming breaths and you feel very good — very confident. When the moment arrives for your presentation, you're pleased to feel yourself walking comfortably to the front of the room — no more wobbly knees or feelings of being faint. You take a confident, comfortable moment before you begin. Looking up at the audience with a warm smile, you feel yourself speaking in a calm, clear, strong voice. You are easily projecting without a hint of nervousness. What a wonderful feeling! Best of all — the applause at the end is spectacular!

You can adapt these scenarios to fit your specific performance situations. In doing so, be certain to make the imaging as close to the physical situation as possible — vivid, detailed, and alive. Place yourself in the scene and be certain to experience the entire situation as if it were taking place now — not at some future date.

This technique is very powerful. Almost always, whenever I took my university students through one of these exercises, they would exclaim at the end, "Wow, that was amazing!" Give it a try.

Mental Rehearsal

Athletes, musicians, and other performers have mastered the preceding technique in enormously effective ways and developed it into what is known as mental rehearsal. This is the process of living a future event as if it were happening now in a kind of rehearsal that even though it is taking place in the mind, is experienced as absolutely alive and real.

I first became aware of the dramatic effect of mental rehearsal many years ago when I was just beginning my research into accelerated learning.

At that time, I read about a study designed by the Australian researcher, Alan Richardson, which focused on mental practice as it applies to basketball. Players were randomly divided into three groups. The first group practiced free throws every day for twenty minutes. The second group, instead of physically practicing the free throws, spent twenty minutes a day visualizing or imagining themselves making the free throws. They were careful to make sure (mentally) that they made the basket, and if not, proceeded to correct the shot. The third group, the control group, did not practice at all. At the end of three weeks, results showed that the group who had physically practiced improved about 24 percent. The group who had not practiced, quite naturally, did not improve at all. But the fascinating result of this study is that the group who practiced only mentally, improved about the same as the group that practiced physically — almost 24 percent. Richardson later commented that the success of those students in the mental practice group was greatly related to how vividly the individual was able image the rehearsal — how well he could visualize the basketball court, "feel" the touch of the ball as well as "see" it, and even "hear" the ball as it bounced.[49]

Eager to learn more about this fascinating process of mental rehearsal with the intention of adapting it for my music students, I contacted the Olympic athletic coach, Dr. Jerry May, whom I mentioned in Chapter IV.

Dr. May, you will recall, had been the Director of Sport Psychology for the U.S. Olympic Training Center in Squaw Valley, California, and has the distinction of having worked with elite athletes and coaches in several sports. He was a wonderful resource! I listened intently as he described to me how he coached the athletes to enter a deeply relaxed, highly suggestive state, and experience performing their sport as if it were taking place. All the senses are brought into play. The ice skaters, for instance, feel their bodies gliding over the ice, hear the sounds of the crowds, feel the cold, hear the blades slicing through the ice — all of it vivid and real. Every movement is performed to perfection — exactly as the athlete directs.

Dr. May's description of how he coaches athletes in the technique of mental rehearsal reminded me of a remarkably similar one I had heard from Dr. Raymond Abrezol as part of a series of lectures on mind/body training which I had recently attended in New York City. Dr. Abrezol had garnered international attention by successfully coaching the Swiss ski team to Olympic gold medals with his mental training techniques.

Now it was all beginning to fit together, and I was excited about applying the principles of mental rehearsal in ways that could benefit my students. However, as generous as Dr. May had been in thoroughly explaining his techniques of mental rehearsal for athletes, he expressed doubt that the same could be applied to music students. For one thing, he was of the opinion that most students lack the discipline and patience required to enter the deeply relaxed physical state with its heightened mental concentration that is required for mental rehearsal to be most effective. He stated that sometimes it takes as long as forty-five minutes for the athletes to reach this state. But I was undeterred, and I set out to apply the techniques of mental rehearsal to the study of music.

Children, Music, and Mental Rehearsal

Not content to let athletes get all the goodies out of mental rehearsal, I eagerly designed a summer project to study the effects of mental rehearsal on learning piano, and fortunately received a research grant to fund the project. I chose to work with nine-year-old children, thinking they would not be as inhibited as older students and more likely to be open to something a little offbeat. I was also of the opinion that younger children had not had their beautiful imaginations squelched by too much formal education. I chose to work with inner city children in this study whom I thought could potentially benefit the most from the mental rehearsal training combined with piano lessons.

After interviewing 56 children nominated by their music teachers, from several inner-city schools, I selected fourteen for the study. And by the way, none of the children had pianos in their homes to use for practice. These fourteen children were driven by bus to the University three mornings a week for a period of six weeks for piano lessons. Half of the children were taught piano traditionally on these mornings for one hour by my assistants. A colleague and I taught the other half of students during the same one-hour period in my piano classroom, but the piano classes were anything but traditional.

From the very beginning, we focused on relaxation exercises with the students in my classroom. In fact, each class session always began with the students pulling the covers over their piano keyboards, resting their heads on the keyboard covers, closing their eyes and listening as I guided them through peaceful, restful, quiet imagery with the soft sounds of Baroque music in the background.

Following the relaxation, it was eyes open, keyboard

covers up, and instruction in the basics of music and beginning piano. The students learned to play little songs on the piano, but the amount of actual piano playing was balanced with an equal amount of mental piano playing — mental rehearsal. We made the mental practicing vivid and fun! They could create their mental pianos any way they wished, in any color they liked — pink, green, bright orange. It could be a cartoon piano that could talk to them. It could be in funny shapes and sizes. They could practice on it anywhere they wished — floating on the water on a sunny day, in a field surrounded by sweet-smelling flowers, riding on a cloud — anywhere they wanted to be with it. Once they had settled in with their very own practice pianos, they imagined playing their little songs perfectly — easily. I was too wrapped up in this fun and fascinating project to even think about taking pictures, but the pictures of those children, deeply relaxed and smiling as they mentally practiced their piano lessons is alive and as vivid in my mind as if it were this morning.

The study worked beautifully! In fact, Sheila Ostrander and Lynn Schroeder documented the research in their book, *Superlearning 2000*, and described the end of our project as follows; "The course finale was a recital joined by children taught traditionally. Independent music judges ranked the now-advantaged children significantly higher than the others as they remembered and played their music with greater proficiency."[50]

Mental Rehearsal in Practice

After the great success of my mental rehearsal/piano study project with those beautiful inner-city children, I began applying the techniques in my college piano classes and with my private students. I began working with the principles myself and received some wonderful results. The main thing for you to realize is that this really works! Practicing anything mentally ahead of time can dramatically improve your performance. You need to keep in mind, however that your ability to relax deeply and to image vividly as if you were performing, is paramount to creating the effect you want. But you can do it! I encourage you to put mental rehearsal to the test if you've never tried. And if you've tried it with little success, keep practicing. It will get better and easier every time you work with it and you can and will receive some terrific benefits!

O━━ **Key 12: Any performance and any situation can be tremendously enhanced through rehearsing it mentally in a state of deep relaxation with vivid imagery.**

Frequently practice lifelike mental rehearsals in a deeply relaxed state to learn and perform easier and better.

Trying Too Hard

It may seem like a confusing contradiction, but in all areas of learning, and particularly in the performance aspect, you can try too hard and interfere with your own accomplishment. "What?" you say, "All I've ever heard from my parents, teachers, coaches, you name it, is that I need to buckle down and <u>try harder</u>." I know. I know. I've heard it too, and most people believe it to be true. However, Dr. Maxwell Maltz points out that all this trying and conscious effort can "jam" our automatic creative mechanism.[51]

> Skill in any performance, whether it be in sports, in playing the piano, in conversation, or in selling merchandise, consists not in painfully and consciously thinking out each   action as it is performed, but in relaxing and letting the job do itself through you.[52]

He goes on, "Excessive carefulness, or being too anxious not to make an error is a form of excessive negative feedback. The result is inhibition and deterioration of performance."[53]

Further insights into this inhibiting feature of "trying too hard" can be found in *The Inner Game of Tennis*, which I mentioned earlier. Timothy Gallwey, a tennis pro made note of the most common complaints that kept coming to his attention from students. Here are a couple:

> "When I'm practicing, I play very well, but when I get into a match, I fall apart." "When I'm really trying hard to do the stroke the way it says to in the book, I flub the shot every time. When I concentrate on one thing I'm supposed to be doing, I forget something else."[54]

Gallwey soon realized that too much conscious trying

was only producing negative results. He began to ask himself, "What's wrong with trying? What does it mean to try too hard?" With those questions in mind, he embarked on a quest to determine the answers. What he discovered was that the mental aspect of any game — any demonstration of learning — was the most important, and that mental aspect needed to be a kind of relaxed effort. In fact, he realized that peak performances come when the player knows where he wants the ball to go, or knows what he wants to happen, but doesn't try consciously to <u>make</u> it happen. He describes this as being "immersed in a flow of action." This is what is meant by the concentrated mind — the mind that is focused on the task without analyzing or thinking about how well we are doing, and not trying to make it happen. But most importantly for us, Gallwey states; ". . . The skill of mastering the art of effortless concentration is invaluable in whatever you set your mind to."[55]

Notice the word "effortless." That just doesn't seem right somehow when we've been instructed otherwise. "Learning is difficult — it takes real effort — we've got to **try hard**."

Does this ring true for you? Do you believe that learning is difficult? Do you have the idea that you must try very hard, not only to learn but to demonstrate that achievement? If so, can you be trying too hard? I believe most of us are trying too hard much of the time. So, what can be done about it?

If you'll think about the imaging exercises in the previous chapter and the powerful ways in which they are able to change our self-image and negative beliefs, why couldn't we use a similar technique to change the pattern of trying too hard?

Here's an exercise I think could be of great help:

Exercise to reverse "Trying Too Hard": Hold the image of what you want to accomplish. See in your mind exactly how you want to perform — the precise outcome you want in vivid detail. Feel as if this outcome is already taking place and you have accomplished exactly what you want in exactly the way you want. Then, as best you can, allow your subconscious to take you there. Don't interfere with this built-in automatic mechanism of your subconscious mind. Relax and let it happen. In other words, don't try!

Throughout this book, we've been looking into the idea that learning is natural and can even be fun. Keeping that in mind, the performance side of learning can be the same when we can learn to relax and let go of the strain and stress. Of course, we've got to put the time in, but with relaxed effort, the whole process becomes easier and when it comes time to perform — to demonstrate what we've learned — we can let go and let it happen.

I witnessed a remarkable demonstration of this by Barry Green at a National Music Teachers Convention. Green, who was the Principal Bassist with the Cincinnati Symphony and Professor of Music at the Cincinnati Conservatory of Music at the time, had adapted Gallwey's tenets to music.

In fact, he had recently published a similar book entitled, *The Inner Game of Music*. Since I had already been studying and working with Gallwey's "inner game" ideas, I was fascinated to see how Green was going to apply them to music. I knew his lecture was going to be fascinating, but I wasn't quite prepared for one particularly striking part of his presentation. In an effort to showcase this concept of creating superior performances through relaxation, Green had invited one of the violinists attending the Convention to perform a short solo for our group. This was a remarkably talented college student and of course we were all appreciative and admiring of her performance. When she finished her playing, and as the applause was dying down, Green escorted the young violinist over to the side of the room and whispered to her for several minutes. You can imagine how intrigued we all were to know what was going on. Eventually, they returned to the center platform and the violinist proceeded to raise her violin with the aplomb of a great master, and performed her solo again, but in a way that was strikingly more exciting. Somehow the performance was more electrifying, thrilling, and I would say even more joyful than the already highly accomplished one we had previously heard. What had Green said to her? He revealed to us that he had simply told the young lady to imagine that she was playing the part of her ideal professional female violinist in a movie. The professional violinist's performance would be dubbed into the movie so she didn't need to worry especially about how she would sound; all she had to do was act like she was playing the violin as would her ideal.

That's it!

I was close to flabbergasted by this demonstration and I decided to test it for myself. During my next summer workshop for music teachers focusing on Accelerated Learning Techniques, I asked one of the participants who was quite an accomplished violist, if she would perform a short solo for the group of teachers. She was puzzled as to why I would request this, but graciously agreed to do it. Following her performance, I took her out into the hallway and essentially told her the same thing that Green had said to his performer. I asked her to think of her favorite female violist — the one whose playing she most admired. She gave me the name and I said, "Fine. Now when we go back in there, I'd like you to perform your solo again as if you are being filmed for a movie on the life of this violist. While you are playing, imagine the sound coming from the other violist playing and that will be dubbed into the movie. You're just playing the role of this performer and don't need to worry about the sound." I admit I was a little nervous because I had no idea if this technique would work again. But to my great delight, and to the astonishment of everyone else attending the workshop, her playing literally soared beyond her previous performance. She even amazed herself!

So what actually happened in these two cases I just described? The soloists had a mental image, a clear mental picture of a highly successful performance. The process involved "No Trying." The performer was engaged in a kind of relaxed concentration, backed by complete confidence — in this case, confidence that the professional sound being dubbed in would be amazing. This sounds a lot like what we've been talking about, doesn't it?

Let's allow ourselves to perform at our best without trying too hard. Let's let it happen!

O━━ Key 13: The secret to a successful performance lies in relaxed concentration, self-confidence, and <u>not</u> trying too hard.

Picture the perfect performance without too much analyzing or trying and allow your very best performance to shine through!

Self-Talk

We all live with something — everyone of us — that we barely recognize. Yet that something is primarily responsible for driving how we perform and to what extent we succeed daily. That something is known as "Self-Talk." Like a hidden but powerful command center, that mental inner voice is dictating how you feel, how you experience yourself, and ultimately how well you are able to perform. Now this would be fine, if that inner voice were chatting up a positive, uplifting, and inspiring tone — cheering you on with an assuredness that creates a solid self-confidence. But sadly, and for reasons beyond the scope of our study here, the vast majority of us experience a daily, incessant onslaught of negative self-talk. This mental soundtrack of negative, sometimes even scolding self-chatter is perhaps the single most inhibiting factor in our ability to perform at our best. How can we possibly fulfill our potential and soar to the heights of our greatest aspirations when this critical inner prattle is crippling our efforts at every turn.

Barry Green calls this "self-interference," and defines it as "the kind of mental static that interferes with our natural ability."[56] Green is so confident of the power of this negative inner talk to inhibit our potential and our performance that he has even come up with an equation to quantify it, which he expresses as follows:

> The basic truth is that our performance of any task depends as much on the extent to which we interfere with our abilities as it does on those abilities themselves. This can be expressed as a formula:
> $P = p - i$
>
> In this equation P refers to Performance, which we define as the result you achieve — what you wind-up feeling, achieving, and learning. Similarly, p stands for potential, defined as your innate ability — what you are naturally capable of. And i means interference — your capacity to get in your own way.[57]

We may not want to admit how deeply and pervasively our inner self talk is interfering with our abilities. But with just a little self-reflection, we can easily identify it. This point became remarkably clear to me during another one of my workshops for music teachers focusing on performance techniques. Rather than simply lecture to the teachers on the role of self-talk in performance, I decided to illustrate it — another idea I received from Green. At the beginning of my lecture, I announced to the group that I would like to perform *Ravel's Pavane pour une infante défunte* on the piano. The group collectively murmured delight — I could hear little comments like, "Oh, how nice, we get to hear her perform." "Have you heard her play?" What the group didn't realize was that this wasn't anything about my performance. It was all about self-talk.

Prior to my presentation, I had recorded some typical examples of extraneous, interfering, negative self-talk that run through a performer's mind. Prior to seating myself at the piano, I hit the play button on the tape player. Now as I adjusted the piano bench, my prerecorded words could be heard; "Boy, am I nervous! I hope my hands don't shake!" Placing my hands on the keyboard, "Why did I wear this dress? I'm sure it makes me look fat." Gradually the giggles started to emerge from the group. As I began playing, "Why did I choose this piece? This piece is so difficult to play. It sounds simple but it's really difficult. Why didn't I choose something that sounds difficult but is really simple?" By now the laughter was beginning to roll. "Oh no, here's that part where I really can't make the stretch! I'll bet I miss it! Yep! I missed it!" At this point, the laughter was so loud that I stopped playing. Why were they laughing? Because every single person identified with the negative self-talk that was accompanying my performance!

Most people realize that success in any performance — music or otherwise — depends on the ability to shut out this negative self-talk and focus our mental efforts on the task at hand. Green states that those times when we perform at our very best ". . . happen when we are mentally alert and aware, but too absorbed in the moment to be running any mental gossip."[58]

So what can we do? Are we stuck with this negative, nagging voice that is determined to keep us from enjoying success and fulfillment? Absolutely not. The encouraging news is that we can deliberately set about to change the negative, judgmental self-talk that inhibits, and puts the brakes on our abilities to perform at our best. But it takes real effort. Are you ready?

Cognitive Restructuring

Although it may seem at times that we are powerless to prevent or eradicate these nagging, negative inner conversations that keep pulling us back and dragging us down, the fact is that we can change those mental talking patterns and create new and life-affirming ones. Psychologists refer to this practice of altering inner self talk as cognitive restructuring. The technique involves deliberately substituting and repeating positive statements in place of the familiar negative ones. We'll examine how we might do this.

However, before we begin the program of transforming our inner dialogue, it might be a good idea to step back and take a day or two just to observe the nature and essence of our habitual self-talk. I think most of us have become so accustomed to our daily inner running commentary, that we have no idea how negative and destructive it could possibly be. Although I must insert here that if you find yourself to be one of those people who fairly skips through the day with nothing but positive, uplifting, lofty, joyful, nurturing and encouraging inner talk, you may equally as well skip this section.

Now, the rest of us. As we were saying, take some time to pay attention to what types of inner comments walk along with you as you go about your activities. What do you hear yourself saying? Do any of these sound familiar:

"You're not going to learn any faster — you never have, and you never will."

"You can try this, but you know it won't work."

"You've tried to improve yourself before and got nowhere."

"This author tries to make it all sound so simple, but let's face it, learning is hard. At least it is for you!"

"Remember the time you worked so hard trying to_____? Remember how that flopped?"

Perhaps your inner commentary isn't quite so straight forward. Maybe it's just little jabs and dabs of self-doubt.

You may say things to yourself like, "Better not take a chance — it's too risky." "You're doing fairly well, don't try to be something you're not."

And then again, your inner dialogue could lean to the opposite extreme: "You're dumb and you know it, and nothing is going to change that!" Severe statements like that are not only wrong, but they're also cruel!

But think about this. These statements are just words — things you have been telling yourself for a long time. They don't have to be true. You can change these statements. You can silence that inner little chatting troll and replace him or her with the kind of inner talk that will absolutely catapult you beyond what you might have thought was even possible.

So where do we start? Once you have identified the nature of your inner thoughts and become aware of how you are talking to yourself — even the exact statements your inner voice tends to repeat — I think it's helpful to write them down. Really get them out there in black and white so that you can stare the words cold-bloodedly in the face — in their ugly face. Then with just as much unemotional determination, write the opposite statement you desire in its place. You may want to write the negative statements on the left of the page and its replacement positive statement on the right. This way you can view what you've been saying, and in the same space see what's going to replace it. You may want to write the negative statement in one color, and the positive in another color

— preferably your favorite. You will deliberately be using these new statements to interrupt and overcome the customary negative ones. You see, you not only want to silence the voice of inhibiting self-criticism; you want to replace it with an equally strong — stronger — voice of encouragement and confidence. Choose positive statements that feel good to you, that seem to resonate with the ideal to which you aspire. This is the new script for your inner dialogue. It doesn't matter whether you believe it. Quite frankly, if your new statements are very positive and you've been repeating negative ones for a very long time, you quite likely won't believe it — at least not a first.

For me, short statements, little phrases that I can repeat over and over many times a day, work better than long statements. I also like to keep the phrases simple — lofty and elevated wording doesn't seem to work as well — at least not for me. Here are a couple of examples:

"This is a new beginning."

"Learning is easier than ever."

"I'm using more of my brain."

"I love learning."

"This really works."

I've also found that rhythmic and rhyming phrases have a special appeal:

"Bright as a dollar, I'm a great scholar."

"Who could foresee, it's so easy for me."

If you really want to punch it up a notch, add emotion to your phrase such as:

"I'm as thrilled as can be, learning's easy for me!"

You can play these phrases over and over in a kind of singsong manner, that has a particularly powerful way of impressing the subconscious mind. I've found that putting the words to a musical phrase or melody that I like, makes the whole process more fun. And I'll give you a little secret, the most profoundly intense way of convincing yourself of a positive change is to insert gratitude into your statement. Create a phase that is a sure sign that you already have the trait you desire and no longer need to keep trying to get it. Repeat this statement and notice how it makes you feel:

"I'm so deeply grateful that I have mastered the Keys to Faster Learning!"

Above all, find the phases that work for you — the statements that feel good to you. Use these new statements deliberately and consciously. Many people have found it helpful to write these statements on notecards and carry the cards with them for reference and reinforcement throughout the day. It's very effective if you can read the statements out loud (if that's possible). In this way you will be seeing and hearing the words, and most importantly feeling the new vibration of positive and encouraging self-talk.

Remember this is your private project. You are

deliberately, with self-determination and great effort, setting out to change your inner dialogue to something that will assure your greatest success in learning easier and faster. I caution you to keep this to yourself—at least in the beginning when your efforts may still be somewhat fragile. You don't want the boot of some naysayer making fun of you stomping out your efforts. Stay with it. I suggest that you pledge to yourself that you will stay with these statements for a minimum of 21 days. I say that, because the general consensus is that it takes 21 days to create a new habit — which more scientifically means that it takes the brain 21 days to establish new neural connections. Committing to this minimum amount of time may be helpful in the beginning, especially if you feel like you're not succeeding in changing your inner dialogue.

Keep repeating the positive statements. You are taking charge of this inner voice. Rather than IT running you, you are dictating the terms and conditions of your inner sound track. After a period of determined effort, you will have succeeded in silencing that negative chatting troll and will have replaced it with a nurturing, kind voice that gives you an uplifting feeling of hope and strength, and ultimately self-confidence. Then, in the moment you're called upon to perform, you can focus all of your energies on the task at hand, free from the constraints of that negative ghoul — free to bring to the fore all that you are. And in that moment, you will astound yourself!

Key 14: Your inner voice is powerfully dictating how well you are able to perform.

Commit to deliberately changing the inner negative self-talk to positive, uplifting words of encouragement and watch yourself perform at your best!

When It's Time to Perform — Relax!

Now it's time to perform: to take the exam, give the presentation, deliver the speech, compete in the sporting event, give the recital — in other words, it's the moment to showcase what you have learned; what you have mastered. So what do you do? You relax and let it happen. You step aside and let your inner self that knows all about it — because of all your preparation — do its thing. It's time to get out of your own way.

This is not the time to frantically study your notes one last time, quickly read the chapters again, rehearse what you're going to say, practice the difficult passage one more time — No! This is the time to put away the notes; forget the last-minute review, practice, or rehearsal. It's time to trust yourself. You can do this now. After all, you realize that your brain is far more powerful than you ever thought possible. You understand the benefits of using your right brain creative imagination along with the left brain's analysis and logic to create more of a whole-brain approach to learning. You're working with a healthier brain because you're exercising and getting all the benefits of that extra oxygen and BDNF — the fertilizer for the brain. You're working with a rested brain through adequate sleep and power naps. You've done the relaxation exercises that help eliminate the stress that interferes with the learning process, and you've learned the benefits of backing off from a problem for a while. You also understand the benefits of relaxing music to center the brain for greater concentration. You're able to use imaging and visualization now in playful, fun, and even outrageous ways to tremendously increase your ability to memorize and recall information. You've done the visualization exercises that help create the outcomes you want. You've successfully learned how to mentally rehearse and prepare for the moment of performance. You've diligently worked on replacing the nagging, negative self-talk with positive and uplifting words that are now allowing you to experience yourself in a far more powerful, confident, and optimistic way. And most importantly, you have a new-found belief in yourself and your own natural abilities that is bound to carry you through to great success.

So now it's time to turn it over to your inner self and allow your subconscious mind to do all the work. Timothy Gallwey emphatically stresses the importance of this by saying, "*Letting* it happen is not *making* it happen."[59] I couldn't agree more.

I'd like to close this chapter with some wonderful sage advice given to me many years ago by an older music professor with whom I served on the same University faculty. She was a wise, elegant, and cultured woman who believed in living life to the fullest. I had gone to her, tense and worried about my upcoming doctoral piano recital, fearful that my nerves might get the best of me, and I would blow the whole thing! (This was long before I'd discovered any of the "learning keys" I've presented in this book.) I knew this talented and sharp-witted woman would have just the right advice — she always did. Here's what she said: "When it comes to performing this is what I do. I practice and prepare as best I can. That is of course the most important thing. When the performance time arrives, just prior to walking out on stage, I say a prayer. As I walk out on stage, I say to myself, 'What the hell!'"

Now, you go prepare using every key on your key ring to make learning faster and easier, and when it's time to perform, relax and Let it Happen!

O—ᴛ Key 15: When you have studied, prepared, visualized, and rehearsed, and it comes time to perform,

<u>Relax and Let It Happen!</u>

Summary

The Keys on Your Key Ring

So now you have the keys — the **"Keys to Faster Learning."** Carry them with you. Write them on note cards. You might even hold them together on an actual key ring. Go over and over each key until its meaning and intent sinks indelibly into your subconscious mind, where all the power is. The keys will work if you use them. In fact, the <u>key</u> to the keys is to apply them to your learning endeavors. Just as one doesn't learn to play the piano by reading about it, the "Keys to Faster Learning" can't work for you unless you practice them. Although many of the keys seem to work magically, this is not just waving a magic wand. You must do the work of using the principles. In other words, it isn't just enough to know about the "Keys to Faster Learning" — how they work — you've got to DO the work and use them. That's when you will really see the magic happen in your own abilities to learn faster.

You might ask me, "Which of these keys do you consider

the most important — the one or two that would help me the most to make learning easier?" Well, in Chapter 6, "The Playful Side of Learning," I referred to the use of the imagination as the "Magic Key to Faster Learning." Certainly, that would indicate that using **Key #10** to associate and image new information vividly and clearly would be one of the most effective. Along with that, we need to include **Key #11** in which you consistently picture and identify yourself as a person who learns quickly and easily as an equally powerful key.

But all of that imaging and visualizing is going to be far more effective when combined with **Key #6**, the use of relaxation exercises to eliminate tension and stress from your body. Quite frankly, just getting into a more relaxed physical state is going to work wonders in creating a heightened, more aware and alert mental state for learning. Allowing your physical body to be centered and completely relaxed is the key that enables your brain to focus and concentrate fully on your learning activity.

But wait, that synchronization of a deeply relaxed body along with a heightened mental awareness is best engendered with **Key #8**, the use of slow Baroque music at 60 beats per minute. In fact, the wave of accelerated learning techniques that began in the early 1980's and was known then as Superlearning, was based on the use of Baroque music as a bridge to induce the kind of relaxed pyscho-physical state in which a relaxed body leaves the mind more alert and easily able to concentrate. And speaking of music, how can we overlook all the studies that indicate listening to the music of Mozart improves attention and performance? Indeed, we need to use **Key #9** which reminds us that not only listening to Mozart, but other slow, relaxing music and even the sounds of nature can increase the brain's ability to learn. Yes, these are two powerful keys which you don't want to overlook.

And of course, we can't leave out **Key #7** and it's almost mystical ability to solve problems by backing off from the problem. You need to keep this key handy for those times when you seem to get stuck. Remember to "Put the Problem Aside" for a time and take regular breaks.

Still, even if you're using all of these keys, they can only be used successfully if you're working with a healthy brain. It is essential that you use **Key #4**, the use of exercise, to boost your brain power, to nourish, and even grow your brain. And you must also use **Key #5**, getting enough sleep and taking naps, not only to ensure that your brain is healthy, but to allow the brain to process and stabilize new information, and get it into useful form. Remember, your brain needs you to sleep <u>before</u> and <u>after</u> learning.

Of course, all of these keys are based on an understanding of how the brain actually works. **Key #2** reminds us that the logical and analytical thinking of the left-brain hemisphere must be integrated with the imaginative and creative aspects of the right brain, to enable the kind of whole brain thinking you need to maximize your full brain potential. But keep in mind, all your best efforts and work in utilizing the "Keys to Faster Learning" are in danger of being squashed if you neglect to remember **Key #14** and the powerful of use of self-talk. You must understand now how vital it is to keep that inner soundtrack in your head speaking positive, uplifting words of encouragement and confidence. Words are powerful — especially the words we choose to speak to ourselves!

And what about those doubts that come up — and they will — that tempt you to dismiss all this faster learning stuff as just claptrap! That's when you're going to need to cling to **Key #1**. A solid grasp of the fact that the brain has greater capacities than we ever dreamed possible can steer you through the mucky thoughts of doubt and insecurity. Remind yourself that this concept of the unlimited potential of the brain isn't just the pep talk of some motivational speaker. It's based on years of solid brain research. When you're tempted to doubt that you can learn easier and faster, get this key out and review the fact that neuroscientists have discovered what is known as brain plasticity — the brain's unique ability to change and improve, and even grow itself through the process of learning. Now that's powerful!

Even when we've mastered and are utilizing all these keys, the time will come when we will be called on to perform — to demonstrate what we have learned. If we've mastered the art of faster learning but choke at the performance, well . . . I don't have to point it out. This is when you've got to grab **Key #12** and mentally rehearse that performance until success is virtually guaranteed. You will need to pair this with **Key #13**, which instructs you to picture and feel that performance going perfectly without trying too hard. And when you have mastered all of this, you can simply put **Key #15** into the lock and turn it by relaxing and letting it happen.

These three keys will work wonders when it's time to perform!

But all of these keys are essentially for the purpose of unlocking the blocks that bring you to the **Master Key**, which when fully turned and accepted can accomplish for you anything you choose. That **Master Key** is **Key #3** and the Power of your own beliefs. When you can get to the place where you believe in yourself, and you know that you not only have the ability, but that you are completely capable of learning — of learning easily, freely, even joyfully — you will have mastered the art of learning. For it is that confidence in yourself, that rock-solid faith in your learning abilities that will unlock the genius within you.

As much as I would like to continue "talking" to you, sharing all that I have learned and experienced in this fascinating journey of faster learning, I realize I must let you go. It's time for you to set sail on this adventure so that you can prove to yourself that you are capable of doing everything we have discussed. You can and will do it!

Now go get busy using all the **"Keys to Faster Learning"** and make your life a joyous adventure! There is so much to learn!!

O—— Key 1: Your brain has a far greater capacity for learning than you ever dreamed possible. The latest research indicates we can improve and grow our brains for even faster and easier learning. Remember this and never allow yourself to feel limited.

O—— Key 2: Integrating the logical and analytical thinking of the left brain with the creative and imaginative capacities of the right brain results in whole-brain thinking. Engage both sides of your brain to dramatically enhance your learning abilities.

O—— Key 3: Our own beliefs powerfully determine how fast we are able to learn. Deliberately change negative and limiting beliefs about your learning abilities to positive ones that will enable you to learn with ease and confidence — often in ways you might never have thought possible.

O—— Key 4: Exercise boosts brain power!! Engage in physical exercise to nourish and grow you brain and learn faster!

O—— Key 5: Sleep greatly increases your ability to learn and retain new information. Get enough sleep, take naps, and learn faster!

O—— Key 6: Relieving stress is a key component to optimal learning. Actively pursue and practice relaxation exercises to learn faster!

O—— Key 7: Letting go or backing off from a problem, can result in new ideas and higher levels of learning performance. When faced with difficulty, remember to "Put the Problem Aside" for a time, take regular breaks, and learn faster!

O—⚷ Key 8: Listening to slow Baroque music can be used to synchronize the mind and body in an ideal state of relaxed and focused awareness, which is the optimal state for learning. Listen to slow Baroque music for several minutes a day while relaxing into a focused awareness and learn faster!

O—⚷ Key 9: Listening to Mozart and other slow music can increase the brain's ability to learn. Listen to Mozart, or some type of slow, relaxing music, or even the soothing sounds of nature every day and learn faster!

O—⚷ Key 10: Associating new information with previous information through imaging greatly enhances the learning process. Image new information vividly, clearly, and even outrageously and learn faster!

O—⚷ Key 11: Our beliefs about our learning abilities powerfully determine the ease with which we are able learn. Limiting beliefs can be changed by impressing the subconscious with new and more positive self- images. Vividly and consistently picture yourself as a person who learns quickly and easily and learn faster!

O—⚷ Key 12: Any performance and any situation, can be tremendously enhanced through rehearsing it mentally in a state of deep relaxation with vivid imagery. Frequently practice vivid mental rehearsals in a deeply

O—⚷

relaxed state to learn and perform easier and better.

O— **Key 13:** The secret to a successful performance lies in relaxed concentration, self-confidence and <u>not</u> trying too hard. Picture the perfect performance without too much analyzing or trying and allow your very best performance to shine through!

O— **Key 14:** Your inner voice is powerfully dictating how well you are able to perform. Commit to deliberately changing the inner negative self-talk to positive, uplifting, words of encouragement and watch yourself perform at your best!

O— **Key 15:** When you have studied, prepared, visualized, and rehearsed, and it comes time to perform, <u>Relax and Let It Happen!</u>

1. Peter Russell, *The Brain Book* (New York: E. P. Dutton, 1979), 7.

2. Norman Doidge M.D., *The Brain That Changes Itself* (New York: A James H. Silberman Book, 2007), xv.

3. Ibid., xiii.

4. Ibid., 47.

5. O'brien, Dominic. *You Can Have an Amazing Memory* (London: Watkins Publishing, 2011), 7.

6. Sheila Ostrander and Lynn Schroeder, *Superlearning* (New York: Dell Publishing Co., 1979), 157.

7. Jim Fannin, *S.C.O.R.E. for Life* (New York: Harper Collins, 2008), 10.

8. Russell, *The Brain Book*, 213.

9. David R. Hamilton, Ph.D., *How Your Mind Can Heal Your Body* (Carlsbad, California: Hay House, INC., 2010), 21-22.

10. O'brien, *You Can Have An Amazing Memory*, 47.

11. Russell, *The Brain Book*, 67.

12. John Medina, *Brain Rules* (Seattle, Washington: Pear Press, 2008), 21-22.

13. John J. Ratey, MD, Spark: *The Revolutionary New Science of Exercise and the Brain* (New York: Little, Brown and Company, 2008), 10.

14. Ibid., 4.

15. Ibid., 13.

16. Ibid., 12.

17. Ibid., 40.

18. Ibid., 44 - 45.

19. Ibid., 114

20. Sara C. Mednick, Ph.D., *Take a Nap! Change your life.* (New York: Workman Publishing, 2006), 33-44.

21. Ibid., 35

22. Ibid., 41-45

23. Ibid., 59-60

24. Sheila Ostrander, and Lynn Schroeder, *Superlearning* 2000 (New York: Dell Publishing, 1994), 53.

25. Maxwell Maltz, *Psycho-Cybernetics* (New York: Prentice-Hall, Inc., 1960), 56-57.

26. Green, Barry, *The Inner Game of Music* (New York: Doubleday, 1986), 213.

27. Arthur Koestler, *The Act of Creation* (New York: Macmillan, 1964), 209.

28. Arthur Koestler, *The Act of Creation* (New York: Macmillan, 1964), 209.

29. Herbert Benson, M.D., and William Proctor, *The Breakout Principle* (New York: Scribner, 2003), 19.

30. Ostrander and Schroeder. *Superlearning* 2000, 31.

31. Don Campbell, *The Mozart Effect* (New York: Avon Books, Inc., 1997), 15.

32. Ibid., 17.

33. Ibid., 27.

34. Ibid., 27.

35. David R. Hamilton, Ph.D., *It's the Thought That Counts* (Carlsbad, California: Hay House, Inc., 2008), 72.

36. Harry Lorayne, *Secrets of Mind Power* (Hollywood, Florida: Frederick Fell Publishers, Inc., 1999), 127.

37. Ibid., 129.

38. O'brien, *You Can Have an Amazing Memory*, 23.

39. Russell, *The Brain Book*, 90.

40. O'brien, *You Can Have an Amazing Memory*, 39.

41. Ibid., 81.

42. Ibid., 81-82.

43. Maltz, *Psychocybernetics*, 49.

44. Ibid., xiii.

45. Hamilton, *How Your Mind Can Heal Your Body*, 39.

46. Bruce H. Lipton, Ph.D., *The Biology of Belief* (Carlsbad, California: Hay House, 2010), 120.

47. Ibid., 120.

48. W. Timothy Gallwey, *The Inner Game of Tennis* (New York: Random House, Inc., 1974), 85.

49. Russell, *The Brain Book*, 215-216.

50. Ostrander and Schroeder, *Superlearning 2000*, 248.

51. Maltz, Psychocybernetics, 77.

52. Ibid., 76.

53. Ibid., 159

54. Gallwey, *The Inner Game of Tennis*, 17.

55. Ibid., 19-21

56. Green, *The Inner Game of Music*, 12.

57. Ibid., 12.

58. Ibid., 14.

59. Gallwey, *The Inner Game of Tennis*, 51.

About the Author

Dr. Linda Ross-Happy has been a university professor for over 35 years, during which time she has distinguished herself as an innovative thinker and researcher in the area of accelerative learning techniques. Her creative research in the use of relaxation and visualization to enhance the learning process was cited in the popular book, *Superlearning 2000*, by Sheila Ostrander and Lynn Schroeder.

The United States Distance Learning Association honored Dr. Ross Happy with the Platinum Award for Excellence in Teaching for her online video course lectures. She is listed in Who's Who Among American Teachers.

Dr. Ross Happy earned her Doctorate from the University of Colorado - Boulder, the Masters degree from Northwestern University, and a Bachelor's degree with distinction from the University of Nebraska - Lincoln where she was named a Ford Foundation Career Scholar. She has held faculty positions at Youngstown State University, Wichita State University, and the University of Missouri - Kansas City.

www.ingramcontent.com/pod-product-compliance
Lightning Source LLC
Chambersburg PA
CBHW030305130626
46549CB00002B/701